Waves of Unreason

Also by John Biggs

Fiction

The Girl in the Golden House

Project Integrens

Disguises

Tin Dragons

From Ashes to Ashes

Black Dog

Towards Forgiveness: Sino-Tasmanian stories from two islands

Non-fiction

Tasmania over Five Generations

Changing Universities

John Biggs

Waves of Unreason

Australian Prime Ministers in the 21st Century

G
P

Waves of Unreason: Australian Prime Ministers in the 21st Century
ISBN 978 1 76041 882 3
Copyright © John Biggs 2020
Cover photo: Patty Jansen from Pixabay

First published 2020 by
GINNINDERRA PRESS
PO Box 3461 Port Adelaide 5015
www.ginninderrapress.com.au

Contents

Introduction

'A wave of unreason' is a phrase author Edgar Wallace used in a 1920s Gothic horror story, wonderfully entitled *The Black Abbot*. I used the phrase in another horror story about a wave of unreason that is currently sweeping the Western world and Australia in particular.[1] I was referring to neoliberalism, the predominant political ideology in Western countries. An updated version of that article appears as Chapter 1, where I discuss how neoliberalism has distorted Australian society, greatly increasing the gap between rich and poor, creating an underclass of people feeling cheated, unwanted and, in some cases, demonised.

The social damage caused by neoliberalism was a perfect breeding ground for populism, seen not only in Australia but in the rise of Donald Trump in the USA, and in the ungovernable chaos after the Brexit referendum in the UK. So, as we in Australia progressed (if that is the right word) into the twenty-first century, we saw many other forms of unreason afflict successive Australian governments and their leaders.

Starting in the Howard years, successive waves of unreason rocked our political system. Labor's dysfunction with the Rudd-Gillard-Rudd succession led us to the Abbott-Turnbull stoushes that left the Liberal party room presented with a choice between two hard right candidates, Peter Dutton and Scott Morrison. They chose Morrison as being more electable. How good was that? Not very, as things are turning out.

While researching and writing this book, I have been shocked by the lying, the aggression, the game playing, the greed, the blind irrationality and the corruption of many of our elected representatives. Australia has been on the wrong track for more than two decades.

Governance has not been in the interests of we the people but in the personal and business interests of too many politicians and their mates, and even of foreign interests.

There surely must be something wrong with a system of government that sees seven prime ministers come and go in twelve years. But worse, out of the last nine elections, seven have been won by the hard-right faction of the Coalition and only two by Labor, when the country is split roughly down the middle between an officially centre right Coalition and centre left Labor. Such an imbalance between election results and the state of the electorate suggests systemic failures that ruthless individuals can exploit only too easily.

The two pillars of the Enlightenment, the ways of reason and of humanity, provide a framework for reflecting on where we are in the current political turmoil. Some structures of government are more effective than others in effectively achieving these priorities, as examined in the final chapter.

*

I am indebted to Lindsay Tuffin, the generous and miracle-working once-editor of *Tasmanian Times*, and Andrew Wilkie MP for his comments. My wife Catherine Tang's editorial eye helped make these essays cleaner than I had left them.

Earlier versions of Chapters 1, 2, 3, and 4 have appeared online at tasmaniantimes.com.

I was inspired in this venture by the fiercely principled Max Bound, with whom I became closely associated in the last years of his politically heroic life. Some of the more important of his writings were published just before his death as *Greed or Survival?* (Search Foundation, 2012). Max's three-word title sums up precisely the dilemma we are facing in the twenty-first century.

John Biggs
Hobart
November 2019

1

The Unreason of Neoliberalism

The way of reason

The Enlightenment saw the Western world start thinking in a way that derives from science, using evidence that is publicly available, and the conclusions drawn therefrom argued logically and transparently. Let's call this the way of reason. Humanism joined the way of reason as summarised in Alexander Pope's *An Essay on Man*:

> Know then thyself, presume not God to scan
> The proper study of Mankind is Man.

Politically, the Enlightenment might have inspired the American Declaration of Independence:

> We hold these truths to be self-evident, that all men are created equal, that they are endowed by their Creator with certain unalienable Rights, that among these are Life, Liberty and the pursuit of Happiness.

These noble words lose some of their lustre when it is pointed out that their principal author, Thomas Jefferson, owned slaves. Nevertheless, the Declaration of Independence is an admirable ideal, giving a broad aim of enlightened governance based on equality. These words have, however, always provided an ideal rather than an actuality, an actuality that today seems to be receding further from the ideal in many Western countries, including Australia.

The other arm of the Enlightenment is the way of reason, which suggests that how to achieve that equality through transparent, evidence-based policy-making that applies equally. No three-word slogans; no people forced to struggle in poverty.

The way of faith

Before the way of reason was the way of faith. We usually associate faith with religious beliefs but it can be faith in any dogma, including political beliefs. Faith is by definition its own validation. Faith is based on authority and its truths are absolute, not evidence-based and provisional as they are in science. The divine right of kings saw the way of faith as the driver of government.

It is a profound and dangerous error to confuse the way of faith with the way of reason. In a speech entitled One Religion is Enough, ex-PM John Howard did just that when he accused those urging action on climate change as forming a new religion acting on faith.[2] Rather than heed the evidence-based conclusion by 97% of climate scientists that drastic action is needed if world temperatures aren't to rise catastrophically, Howard preferred to rely on his 'instinct': 'I instinctively feel that some of the claims are exaggerated,' he said.

He was the one acting on faith. He was asserting that the inner feelings of one individual – himself – carried a higher priority in making public policy than independently validated findings from science. That is a breathtaking act of faith in one's own private data bank, a source that is inaccessible to anyone else. Does such self-faith verge on the pathological?

In Western democracy, the separation of religion from politics should be well established. Yet Tony Blair actually ordered his staff on one occasion to pray at the end of a meeting: 'I said: "You'll have to get on your knees." One of them said: "For God's sake" and I said: "Exactly."'[3]

George Bush claimed that he conferred with God before making decisions. Did God then suggest that Bush should invade Iraq at the cost of hundreds of thousands of Iraqi lives and untold other damage, including that to his own troops and their families? I don't know if Tony

Blair or John Howard, Christians both, also sought God's advice when they joined forces with their friend George in this crime against humanity. The fact is that the war was engaged by three men who publicly professed their Christianity when that religion's prime exhortation is 'love your neighbour' and 'peace on earth and goodwill towards men'.

But Australia in 2018–19 even exceeds these conflations between religion and politics with the prime ministership of Scott Morrison. This entanglement is explained in Chapters 5 and 6.

The rise of soft neoliberalism

Neoliberalism shaped policy in Australia much earlier than Abbott or Howard. When Bob Hawke came to power in 1983, the government set the level of interest rates, of the Australian dollar and tariffs, while wages were set centrally by the Industrial Relations Commission. When Labor left office in 1996, the government had virtually abolished tariffs, had ceded control over interest rates to an independent Reserve Bank, and the value of the dollar and wages to market forces, and had privatised the Commonwealth Bank and Qantas. The Hawke-Keating government reduced corporate taxes from 49 to 33 cents in the dollar, and the personal tax rate from 60 cents maximum to 47 cents. The wages share of GDP fell from around 61.5% of GDP to less than 55%, which amounted to a transfer of $50 billion from workers to the already very rich. Thus was created the biggest transformation in the Australian economy since World War II, achieved by deregulating controls over business and letting market forces rule. When Keating brought in compulsory superannuation, people's super funds were locked into the stock market, forcing them to be party to preserving the dangerous neoliberal desideratum of annual growth (see below). While the middle class are in real terms wealthier today than they ever were, an underclass of unemployed and underprivileged people is very much poorer.

These changes, by a Labor government, severely weakened the unions and eroded Labor's own support base in the working class.[4] Labor might have a stated socialist objective in its constitution:

The Australian Labor Party is a democratic socialist party and has the objective of the democratic socialisation of industry, production, distribution and exchange, to the extent necessary to eliminate exploitation and other anti-social features in these fields.

But these are only words. In practice, Labor after Hawke-Keating operated mainly as a neoliberal government for the corporate benefit, rather less so for the benefit of their traditional constituents. Only in 2019 did Labor try to return to its democratic socialist values. They failed. That cautionary tale is told in Chapter 6.

Keating later got the nearest he could to admitting to a mistake. In 2017, when it was glaringly obvious that neoliberalism was dividing the nation more and more into rich and poor, causing ACTU leader Sally McManus to assert that 'neoliberalism had run its course'. Keating agreed, if a bit late in the day:

> Liberal [that is, neoliberal] economics had [in the past] dramatically increased wealth around the world…but since 2008, liberal economics has gone nowhere… We have a comatose world economy held together by debt and central bank money. Liberal economics has run into a dead end and has had no answer to the contemporary malaise.[5]

Keating may have been instrumental in introducing neoliberalism in the 1980s, but when the Liberals achieved government in 1996, they out-Keatinged Keating by far.

Enter hard neoliberalism

Our two-party system was designed in a simpler world to offer two distinct alternatives to the electorate – right representing employers and the economy, and left representing employees and workers' rights. Both accepted the need for a social welfare system. John Howard in his election as PM in 1996 turned his back on classical Liberalism, despite his adulation of Bob Menzies, and showed us what hard neoliberalism was about.

Neoliberal governments minimise the regulation of business, leaving major economic, political and even social decisions for the 'Market' to make, as if that reified abstraction could possibly make decisions. No, the decisions are made not by this Market thing at all, but by those who dominate trade in goods and increasingly in meta-goods such as stocks, shares and bonds, which generate their own super-wealth. In fact, this latter trade far exceeds the trade in goods and labour, to the severe disadvantage of the workforce and to the huge advantage of the already super-rich who use their money to make more money.[6]

Leaving it to this Market really means leaving it to corporations to maximise their profits, which rise at a much faster rate than do wages. The result is an explosion of wealth upwards to the already rich, company CEOs getting paid obscene salaries, such as Qantas chief Alan Joyce receiving $23 million in 2019 alone. The redistribution of this new wealth relies not so much on taxes, which are minimised especially at the higher brackets, but on a presumed trickle-down effect: rich people buy more things, which means more employment for the less privileged, like shop assistants. Lucky shop assistants.

Margaret Thatcher in discussing market economics famously said, 'TINA! There is no alternative." Yes, there is an alternative: that foreshadowed by the Enlightenment, a polity in which all citizens are equal and have rights to life, liberty and happiness, pursued as best thought possible by representatives of the people making informed decisions on the basis of known facts and science.

But that is not the way neoliberalism works. When the great majority of climate scientists warned us that we were creating danger- ous climate change because of unregulated growth yielding carbon and methane emissions, ex-Prime Minister Tony Abbott said that man-created global warming was 'absolute crap', and that 'coal is good for humanity'. In other words, he thought that the creation of wealth by the few, who donate large amounts to the Liberal Party, was a higher priority than the welfare of the many, even of the planet itself.

Subsequent prime ministers Turnbull and Morrison continued this honoured Liberal tradition.

From the Howard years onwards, the electorate had a choice between neoliberal hard (Liberal) and neoliberal soft (Labor). The many who do not agree with neoliberalism were therefore not adequately represented in our so-called representative democracy. Consequently, governments over the past twenty years had become increasingly out of touch with the electorate. Minor parties and independents representing both left and right blurred what was once a solid two-party system. It is only in the last couple of years that the Labor Party has tried to distance itself from the excesses of Coalition policy (except on asylum seeker policy and so-called national security issues) and resurrect a trace of its traditional values.

The Keating legacy

But the damage wrought by Hawke and Keating when they vaulted to the other side of the fence wasn't only limited to their implementing neoliberal policies. Keating's rhetoric, sometimes uplifting, frequently vile, set new standards of mutual disrespect amongst politicians. On Howard: 'this little desiccated coconut', 'a dead carcase swinging in the breeze'; on Costello: 'all tip and no iceberg'; on Andrew Peacock: 'we're not interested in the views of perfumed, painted gigolos', 'can a soufflé rise twice?' and much more. Witty, funny, but did this sort of invective pave the way for the later unwitty and unfunny epithets such as 'Juliar', 'ditch the witch', 'Bob Brown's bitch', 'Bill Shorten's a liar; he always lies'? Did it sanction the poisonous hurling of insults that replaces reasoned debate in Parliament and, worst of all, wins elections as it did in 2019?

Another piece of nastiness that Keating introduced, with bipartisan support, was the mandatory detention of asylum seekers in 1992. Thus, on economic policy, denial of human rights and uncivilised parliamentary behaviour, Paul Keating can be held to have laid the unpleasant foundations upon which Howard, Abbott, Turnbull and Morrison gleefully built.

Nevertheless, Keating also had a social conscience, as exemplified in his Redfern speech, the Mabo decision, and several policies upholding human rights – but he was inconsistent, as his mandatory detention policy testifies. Keating was a Third Way politician, like Bill Clinton and Tony Blair. They tried to blend varying syntheses of left and right policies. Keating's Third Way, like Blair's in England, only resulted in an uneasy compromise that confused what Labor really stood for.

The four concerns of good government

A fair and fully functioning government needs to address at least four areas of concern for a well-balanced society: economic growth, social justice, environmental sustainability, and being a good global citizen. Under neoliberalism, economic growth is given top priority over the other three areas of concern. Annual growth based on low tax regimes is socially unjust, environmentally damaging and bad global citizenship when, for example, underpaid foreign workers are exploited under limited working visas. Labor at least tries to incorporate social justice into its platform – apart from asylum seekers – but it is difficult because neoliberalism is simply incompatible with social justice.

The neoliberal commitment to privatisation places corporate above community interests. Privately run businesses can sometimes be more efficient and less of a drain on the public purse than government run, but frequently the results in terms of public welfare are unacceptable. When the Sydney Water Board was corporatised in 1994, thousands of jobs were lost and household water prices doubled in a few years. Water bills for big business on the other hand dropped by an average of 45% in real terms. Safety and monitoring services were reduced because they are expensive, resulting in dangerous increases in giardia and cryptosporidium contamination. It is obvious why. When service functions are privatised, priorities change: from serving the public to maximising profits and shareholders' dividends. Typically, privatisation results in the accumulation of private wealth to the detriment of the public interest.

Neoliberal governments are committed to their policies as an act of faith. Thatcher's 'TINA' was as fervent as the cry of any fundamental evangelist. And today we have a prime minister who is a fervent evangelist for prosperity theology, where wealth is seen as God's blessing on His chosen. Just the sort of religion that neoliberals would love.

Unreason in recent Australian politics

Italian philosopher Antonio Gramsci explained why people vote against their own interests with the concept of 'cultural hegemony'. This is achieved by relentless spin and name-calling and by appealing to common sense rather than to good sense.[7] Thus it is touted as common sense, to which all sensible people would surely agree, that the economy must grow annually. But this is not good sense at all: an economy based on non-renewable resources can't grow exponentially. The law of the conservation of matter sees to that.

Gillard's Labor government was given negative saturation by the press in a way that distorted reality. News Ltd, which owns two-thirds of daily and Sunday papers and the only papers in Brisbane and Hobart, was essentially a propaganda machine for the Liberal Party. Little or nothing was said about Labor's achievements, which were considerable. For example, one of the initiatives that saw us through the GFC, the pink batts scheme, resulted in four deaths on site, an accident rate not at variance with the industrial rate generally. Yet the Liberals, with support from the press, painted that as massive Labor incompetence and set up a Royal Commission to investigate the 'mishandling' of the scheme. And it worked. People voted for the Abbott government in disgust at Labor's apparent dysfunction. Since then, we have had six years of Coalition government and two more prime ministers who achieved very little except even more dysfunction.

Richard Dennis's *Econobabble*[8] explains with marvellous clarity how conservative politicians misuse economic-sounding concepts to peddle neoliberal policies that are very much against the interests of ordinary Australians.[9] The mining controversy is an example. Politicians and mining magnates claimed that royalties and taxes from the mining boom financed schools and hospitals. Maybe a little, but most of the bonanza was used to finance tax cuts for the rich – corporate management and shareholders – not public welfare. It also pushed the dollar up by 50% to over US$1, seriously damaging the non-mining business sector. Tourism and manufacturing and other exports actually lost more than the mining sector paid into the economy. When you factor in the massive subsidies in the form of government-paid roads, the diesel rebate, rail and other infrastructure, we discover that mining has taken from the economy rather more than it has given. When the mining boom busted, as booms tend to do, the West Australian government was left empty-handed and Liberal Premier Colin Barnett out of a job.

More unreason. Abbott, Turnbull and Morrison pushed the Indian-owned Adani mine in Queensland, despite the huge addition to carbon emissions, the danger to the hugely important Great Artesian Basin for agriculture, to the Great Barrier Reef, to endangered species, to the fact it offers much fewer jobs than originally claimed, to wrecking Aboriginal sacred land sites, and to the not inconsiderable fact that most profits would flow overseas (see pages 64–65).

Unreason and climate change

Climate change action is probably the worst example of unreason on both sides of politics. In the 1970s, scientists began warnings about man-induced climate change, so that thirty years later the need to mitigate greenhouse gas emissions was seen by a majority of people and many politicians as a top priority. But this meant moving away from fossil fuels into renewable sources of energy. In many countries, and briefly in Australia, a price was put on carbon, which was widely agreed to be the most effective weapon against climate change.

However, the mining and fossil fuel industries, massive donors to both parties but especially to the Nationals and Liberals, fought back. The industry rustled up a few rogue scientists, some with connections with the industry and none being climate scientists, loudly demanding that these nonclimate scientists be given equal time with the climate specialists. Murdoch's News Ltd played a scurrilous role in this: 97% of the columns appearing in the *Herald-Sun* were sceptical of human-caused global warming, a symmetrical reflection to the 97% of scientists who concluded the very opposite. People became deeply confused, and when carbon pricing was called 'a great big toxic tax', it was game over, a massive win for unreason. Under this sort of pressure, Rudd squibbed attending to what he saw as 'the greatest moral challenge of our time' (see pages 32–35). That catastrophe of inaction lasted over ten years and into the Morrison government.

The Coalition agreed that some plan was politically necessary but preferably one that wouldn't work. Accordingly, Morrison rebadged Abbott's ineffectual 'Direct Action' as 'Climate Solutions', a misnomer if ever there was one. Morrison's version would pay $2 billion, instead of Abbott's $3.6 billion, directly to polluting industries if their pollution decreased. Here was a scheme built for rorting. And carbon emissions kept right on rising.

Gillard's Clean Energy Finance Corporation (CEFC) obtained private sector investors to invest in renewable energy projects that not only decreased carbon emissions but made big money, some $3 billion in short order. And isn't that what neoliberalism is about? Yet Abbott eyed it balefully. His death thrust was largely, perhaps entirely, because the CEFC was created by the Gillard government. Fortunately, that shiver of madness was recognised as such by the Senate, who blocked Abbott's legislation to dismantle the CEFC.

When Abbott was PM, he vowed to abolish everything Labor had put in place. He abolished the portfolio of Minister for Science, reduced Australian Research Council funding, and cut almost a quarter of scientists, researchers and workers at the Commonwealth Scientific and Industrial Research Organisation, Australia's premium research body.

The Paris United Nations Climate Change Conference in

November–December 2015 was the biggest demonstration so far that the climate issue had at last been recognised by almost all countries, and that something had to be done about it. However, some countries, like Australia, added the caveat that such action must not harm the economy. Agreement between 196 parties was reached to aim for specific target figures of reduced carbon emissions, with the targets of only three countries being smaller than Australia's. However, the means of achieving these targets, and any sanctions for failing to do so, were not clear. General consensus was for some form of carbon pricing – a good neoliberal mechanism using market forces – which makes Direct Action/Climate Solutions even more odd coming from neoliberal governments. Our inability to handle climate change is a recurrent theme in these pages.

In a bizarre sequel to the Paris conference, at a World Government Summit in Dubai sponsored by a consortium of fossil fuel industries, the prime minister of the UAE awarded Environment Minister Greg Hunt the title of 'World's Best Minister' for his efforts towards protecting the environment. As Hunt had been Abbott's main saboteur in destroying anything effective against climate change, Hunt had indeed been protecting the environment – that of the fossil fuel industry.

Neoliberalism and democracy

Neoliberalism leads to a far greater disparity of wealth both within and between countries. If democratic processes slow down neoliberal reforms, which frequently happens, neoliberal governments sidestep democracy. It is standard corporate practice, with the help of corrupt governments, to take advantage of cheap resources, both human and material, in underdeveloped countries, in the course of which locals are often deprived of water, agricultural land, habitat and their way of life. And most frequently the massive profits go offshore.

Another example of sidestepping democracy is the Trans Pacific Partnership (TPP), which includes an Investor-State Dispute

Settlement (ISDS) clause. These clauses give corporations the right to sue member countries for loss of profit occasioned by national legislation. Australia agreed to including ISDS clauses even while Philip Morris was in that very process of suing Australia over plain packaging! How's that for unreason, once-Minister Andrew Robb? Fortunately, Philip Morris's claim was later rejected by a Singapore court, and the World Trade Organisation is billed to reject claims by several tobacco growing countries that the plain packaging laws are illegal barriers to trade.

This ISDS clause is only available to corporations, not to citizens of the nations who are party to the agreement. One tribunal judge reportedly said, with regard to the clause,

> It never ceases to amaze me that sovereign states have agreed to investment arbitration at all... Three private individuals are entrusted with the power to review, without any restriction or appeal procedure, all actions of the government, all decisions of the courts, and all laws and regulations emanating from parliament.[10]

And it never ceases to amaze thinking citizens that their governments could sell them down the river like that.

In 2004, the USA and Australia signed a free trade agreement and in the following year, Australian exports to the US declined, while US exports to Australia increased. The IMF predicted that the Australia–United States FTA would shrink the Australian economy because of the loss of trade with other countries – that loss was $US56 billion in 2012 alone, with losses each year from 2005, according to an Australian National University study.[11] Yet the Coalition government signed up for further losses by more free trade! Business editor Ian Verrender clarifies what that was all about:

> The TPP was an American foreign policy initiative to counter the influence of China around the Pacific rim. Add in a few onerous clauses that would advance the interests of American corporations, particularly the pharmaceutical giants and Silicon Valley, and it

was a deal that spelled sweet success for Washington. The fact that Mr Trump pulled the pin on a deal that favoured America tells you all you need to know about the President and his administration.[12]

Australia signed the Trans Pacific Partnership Free Trade agreement, but fortunately Donald Trump refused to sign on the grounds that the TPP didn't do enough for America. PM Turnbull tried to revive the TPP minus the USA as the Comprehensive and Progressive Agreement for Trans-Pacific Partnership (CPTPP). The deal was signed, without the US, in March 2018.

The Chinese Free Trade Agreement (ChFTA) is another example of such unreason. Tasmania is a major producer of milk products and of top seafood, and China has massive appetites for both, with buying power to match. Thus, local markets are likely to be starved of local produce and what there is will be rather more expensive than hitherto. And if that's not enough, a Chinese company was allowed to buy the Van Diemen's Land Company, the biggest dairy farm in Australia. It is all in the interests of free trade, you see. And in that game, the biggest player wins. And that is not Australia, and certainly not Tasmania.

Although Australia has the world's largest natural gas resources, neoliberal free trade agreements allow producers to sell to the highest bidder, which most frequently means overseas. Yet we desperately need gas at home, which is in such short supply that Australians now pay nearly twice as much for their gas as Japan pays for Australian gas! That is not unreason in terms of market economics, but it is for governments to have allowed it to happen.

Economically, neoliberalism has generated a financial system that is running out of control. Post GFC, the situation has become even more unstable. Speculative derivatives, that are very high risk, trade mainly between Wall Street and the City of London at the rate of US$4 trillion every day, of which Australia alone trades AUD$41 billion a day. These trading decisions are automated and made within microseconds, beyond any human monitoring or control.[13]

The Global Financial Crisis came about because the banks grossly over-lent on unsecured mortgages. Commentators believed at the time that such greed-driven stupidity would spell the collapse of neo-liberalism. However, those responsible weren't punished; they were charged with fixing the very problem that they themselves had created. Instead of government taking the pressure off the people whose mort-gages were now unmanageable, hundreds of billions of dollars of tax-payers' money were used to prop up the failed private banks. It would have been far cheaper and better for the banks themselves, John Ralston Saul argues, if the government had taken over those mort-gages.[14] People would then have money to keep the economy going and the banks would have remained sustainable. But instead of ques-tioning the economic theory that had led to the global financial crisis, the solution to the problem was more of the same – to everyone's detri-ment except for the extremely wealthy few whose greed had created the problem.

The end of neoliberalism? Not quite yet it seems

Richard Denniss believes that neoliberalism has 'eaten itself' so he is considering what comes next.[15] Denniss points out the unfairness, the inconsistencies, the counterproductive outcomes and much else that is wrong with neoliberalism such that it will bring about its own demise. He says that neoliberalism is dead in the sense that the political proponents of neoliberalism don't actually believe in it any more. They are simply using this ideology as a cloak behind which they can conceal the fact that they love giving public money to their friends and that they love using red tape and regulation to tie their enemies up in knots. If the Coalition was truly neoliberal, why would they want to nationalise coal mines and coal-fired power stations? If Denniss is right, then that sort of greed and blatant dishonesty cannot indeed survive.

Denniss suggests that democratising the existing structure will occur: providing a bill of rights, increasing rates of tax for the highest incomes both individual and corporate, replacing the Productivity Commission, which is solely business-focused, with a broader

National Interest Commission, establishing a corruption watchdog at federal level, and a sovereign wealth fund like Norway's. The latter is a very large sock in which prodigious North Sea oil profits are stashed away in sensible investments as a buffer for the future, whereas Howard and Costello dissipated mining profits in tax cuts that benefited the rich. Denniss's optimism is yet to be realised in Australia.

It is true that many people are highly sceptical of the effects neoliberalism are having on their lives. Grass roots protest groups, such as People's Global Action, the Occupy Movement, Lock the Gate Alliance, GetUp! and many more, are making their presence felt, especially through social media. They have had some victories, especially in stalling fracking and some mining projects, but in the long run these interventions amount to putting out spot fires.

Neoliberalism, instead of self-destructing, laid the foundations for something worse: populism. Terrorism, mass immigration and consequent feelings of outrage have in their various ways shifted some countries to vote in far-right governments whose economic policies created the poverty and other problems that caused millions to emigrate, which in turn continues a cycle of hatred and destabilisation.

Now for alt-right populism

Populism in politics may sound good, if it means governing for what the people seem to want, but it doesn't mean that. In a properly working representative democracy, government serves all the people – young, old, immigrant, indigenous, poor, rich – with equal fairness. Neoliberalism, however, favours the rich and the corporate world against ordinary people, and that is the starting point for an even more vicious perversion of government.

Neoliberalism sets the scene for an alternative right (alt-right) populism. Under neoliberalism, the poor feel disenfranchised, powerless, and deeply resentful against the elites who are oppressing them. Then along comes someone who seems to identify with them and vows to fight those dreadful elites. Donald Trump's takeover of the White

House is a classic example of how populism works. He identified the 'elites' as Them – super-rich Democrats like the Clintons, who turned the White House into 'a swamp' that he alone could drain. The elite included academics, the media, judges and the law courts – indeed anyone with whom ordinary Americans wouldn't identify. These elites were said to have done all sorts of terrible things: they came after your money, they shut down manufacturing and associated jobs, they allowed immigrants to steal jobs from honest Americans. Trump built up his support base, who worshipped him because he played on their greatest fears and hatreds. Wherever he could, Trump stacked the courts and senior administrative positions with his own supporters and acolytes, including his own family, giving him far more power than should be held by the president.

Australia is not there yet but there are signs, as Greg Barns points out.[16] Howard started populist strategies with *Tampa*, when he flouted international law by refusing permission for refugees to land in Australia. He claimed to be on side with 'the Aussie battlers' – in this case, racists in swinging seats – and against latte-sipping elites. He was regularly on shock jock Alan Jones's populist breakfast show, even making policy announcements there rather than from government sources or from the ABC. Abbott did likewise but he had his own weird agenda that blew up on him. Scott Morrison played the populist card for all it was worth, referring to coal-produced electricity as 'fair dinkum power', wearing hi-vis vest and hard hat on any remotely relevant opportunity, using broad Australian slang and continually mouthing about his football team the Sharks and generally playing the dinki-di ocker Australian: a loveable daggy dad. But not so lovable as things turned out, as we see in Chapters 5 and 6.

The flip side of cosseting up to Us is how you treat Them. In Australia, Them comprise Aboriginals, immigrants, other ethnicities in general, and the poor and disadvantaged. Thus, the Turnbull government flatly ignored the Uluru Statement from the Heart, despite the government having asked Indigenous Australians for their advice on how they might play a bigger part in Australian politics. Morrison, then Dutton, insulted asylum seekers as paedophiles, terrorists and whatever else suited them to say, that Muslims didn't integrate to became Australians, that South Sudanese youth were terrorising Melbourne diners in inner-city restaurants. One outcome of splattering all this hatred around was the Christchurch massacre in which an Australian, thus stoked with ethnic hatred, fired on two Christchurch mosques killing fifty people and injuring fifty others.

Individuals who seemed 'un-Australian' were attacked. Yassman Abdel-Magied, a female Muslim journalist, who made a not unreasonable comment about Nauru and Manus Island on her Facebook in the context of Anzac Day, was roasted so badly by hard right politicians and the press that she left the country. Human Rights Commission President Gillian Triggs was doing her job in monitoring human rights on Nauru and Manus, which is precisely why Abbott and the Murdoch press crucified her. The United Nations is anathema to the right: Dutton assured us we were not going to sign any document that is not in Australia's interests, such as a climate policy or asylum seeker protection. Abbott assured us we were 'sick of being lectured to by the UN'.

I go into more detail about this phase in our politics in later chapters. The present point is that whereas neoliberals brought unreason to the economy, alt-right populism brings unreason to society in general.

Unreason and post-truth politics

Had we not pushed for relentless growth in a carbon-based economy, had we not invaded Iraq, or chopped up and redistributed the Middle East in the last century, but paused for reasoned and careful thought about consequences, the negative effects of neoliberalism and alt-right populism would be very much less than they are today.

In July 2014, John Connor had described Tony Abbott's handling of the carbon tax debate as the 'nadir of post-truth politics'.[17] Malcolm Turnbull actually moved from an evidence-based and considered position on handling climate change to a cowardly and mendacious one. But Morrison beat both on post-truth politics: he ran an entire election campaign on outrageous lies.

The US elections showed that post-truth politics is the new normal, Oxford Dictionaries even declaring 'post-truth' as the word of year for 2016. Professor Carl-Henrik Heldin, chairman of the board of the Nobel Foundation, said,

> Leading politicians – both in Europe and the United States – are winning votes by denying knowledge and scientific truths. Populism is widespread and is reaping major political successes. The grim truth is that we can no longer take it for granted that people believe in science, facts and knowledge.[18]

We are now living in a world of unreason that in many significant ways is approaching that of pre-Enlightenment days.

2

Howard's End: The Rudd-Gillard-Rudd Fiasco

The downfall of the dullest man

On being elected prime minister in 1996, John Howard was threatened on the right by Pauline Hanson's racist One Nation Party. He soon fixed that by gobbling up her policies, thus taking his own party even further to the right. Against the odds, he went to the 1998 election with the promise of a GST, which nearly lost it for him. The Coalition got fewer votes than Labor but more seats. Howard didn't have the Senate, though, and the Democrats who had the balance of power were elected on an anti-GST platform. Howard negotiated for nearly three days with Meg Lees, the Democrat leader. Being locked up with Howard must have been an increasingly unpleasant experience for her, because she capitulated, with some concessions in the final bill. Neoliberal policy had won; the Democrats were broken as a credible party. Thank you, Meg Lees.

Labor looked set to win the 2001 election but was stymied by two factors. The first was the *Tampa* affair, when a Norwegian freighter picked up 438 asylum seekers from a distressed vessel. Howard would not allow the *Tampa* into Australian waters, and although this was clearly in violation of international law, it went down big with racist voters in swinging seats. Kim Beazley, Labor opposition leader, meekly followed Howard's lead, the effect of which was to further compound Labor's policy confusions.

The second factor that saved Howard was the attack on the World Trade Centre on 11 September 2001. This was a gift to conservative governments generally, given their bellicose tendencies and the massive insecurity this attack engendered in the West. George Bush's popularity grew to a massive ninety%, in which Howard basked, as a friend of Bush.

Howard's next boost came when George Bush decided to go to war on Iraq. Howard was in Washington at the time, and entirely off his own bat immediately pledged Australian support for the US invasion of Iraq. The US motivation for the Iraq War was ostensibly to disarm Iraq of weapons of mass destruction, when the best validated advice was that such weaponry did not exist. Andrew Wilkie, of the Office of National Assessments and an intelligence analyst, and international weapons inspector Hans Blix, agreed: there were no weapons of mass destruction in Iraq.

Which brings us to the real reasons for invasion: to grab Iraq oil, and to destroy the infrastructure of publicly owned water and utilities so they could be privatised and taken over by Vice President Cheney's corporation Haliburton. None of this was any of Australia's business yet Howard pledged Australian support for Bush's invasion of Iraq with no reference to Parliament. He well knew that a great majority of Australians were against any such war. It says much about Labor's lack-lustre appeal under new leader Mark Latham that, despite the Iraq atrocity, Howard as Bush's 'man of steel' won the next election.

Howard's downfall came in the 2007 elections. Howard, now in command of the Senate, introduced the deeply unpopular Work Choices, a bill that severely disadvantaged workers. That clinched it. He lost the 2007 election and his own seat to Maxine McKew.

Bill Bryson was rather naughty as a visiting commentator when he wrote,

John Howard is by far the dullest person in Australia. Imagine a very committed funeral home director whose burning ambition from the age of eleven was to be a funeral home director... Then halve his personality and halve it again, and you have pretty well got John Howard.[19]

After eleven dreary years of him, voters were tired of their dull as dull funeral home director.

Maxine McKew enters Parliament

After years as a highly respected political reporter, Maxine McKew, in *Tales from the Political Trenches*, described how she wanted to be a player in politics not a 'voyeur', as Keating had put it to her. She was approached by the right faction NSW to have a safe seat in the 2004 election but in return they demanded her loyalty to that faction. Disgusted, she wanted to be beholden to nobody, except to Kevin Rudd, who she greatly admired at the time.

Her husband, Labor veteran Bob Hogg, suggested she put herself forward in the 2007 election for Howard's seat in Bennelong. She ran an intense but clean campaign, specifically avoiding disparaging her opponent and won, thereby making political history: a newcomer defeating an incumbent prime minister. Rudd and his team won in a landslide in 2007, the size of their victory making more political history.

Once in parliament, however, McKew didn't see much of Rudd: he was frenetically busy. His office posted dot-point phrases all politicians had to echo when talking to the press, inevitably making them sound robotic and insincere. McKew had plenty of good things to say about her field of early childhood education and said so to the *Sydney Morning Herald*. At six a.m. next morning, Rudd's minder Lachlan Harris was on the phone blasting her for daring to talk outside the guidelines for the day. She had thought servile obedience was not what politics was about but that doing a good job within your remit was. Lachlan Harris was quick to try to put her right on that one.

She had been looking forward to participating in a contest of ideas, which Keating had told her was what politics was all about, only to discover that MPs of less than ministerial status had little or no input. Instead, Rudd, Gillard, Swan and Lindsay Tanner – the Gang of Four – were running things by themselves. Ministers outside this so-called 'kitchen cabinet' might present their case for a given policy within their area but were excluded when a decision was being taken. McKew was also shocked at the power the faction leaders had: she described them as 'apparatchiks whose aim was self-advancement' and who seemed unconcerned about the good of Australia – even about the good of the party, as later events showed. Rudd, like McKew herself, was atypical in the ALP in that neither had a union background and were not beholden to any factions. This, she says, was a major reason why Rudd was deposed.

McKew found she didn't like the way politics was played. The real enemy, she was told early in her parliamentary career, was more likely to be sitting beside her rather than on the opposite benches. Competition was a fierce zero-sum game: your promotion meant that someone had lost. To get on, you had to have a 'look at me profile, ask shrill even silly questions, denounce the opposition in the media, but never deviate from the orders of the day'.

Maxine's criticisms about the power of factions still apply, despite that power being hated by the electorate. For example, Lisa Singh, a particularly effective Labor Senator but not aligned to any faction, was placed at fourth position of the Labor Senate ticket by the powerbrokers in the 2016 election. That enraged many Labor and non-Labor voters to the extent that she made electoral history by being elected to the Senate despite having been placed an unwinnable fourth on the ticket. Learning nothing, the factional heavies again placed her fourth on the 2019 Senate ticket. Although she gained 20,000 personal votes below the line, much the same as in 2016, and more than any other Tasmania senator, she was defeated by factional preferences.

Those two sorry episodes did Tasmanian state Labor serious harm in the public eye.

Rudd's 'ambush'

As for what she calls the 'ambush', meetings of the chief conspirators – mainly Gillard, Swan, Mark Arbib, Paul Howes and Bill Shorten – had been ongoing since January 2009, six months before Rudd's 'knifing'.

McKew was outraged. If Rudd was as bad as his erstwhile colleagues had claimed, she finds it incredible that not one minister had the guts to warn Rudd to lift his game or there might be a takeover. She says, 'It is surely beyond tolerable that a modern party can have its fortunes determined by half a dozen largely trade union leaders who see themselves as more influential than the party's elected parliamentarians.' Outside this cabal, a majority of the party sided with Gillard but several admitted later to McKew that they had been misled and manipulated; in retrospect, they had deeply regretted that they had voted Rudd out.

McKew's view, like that of many others, was that Rudd had won a massive victory in 2007, his approval rating in the polls at 66%. He made the long-awaited apology to indigenous Australians, ratified the Kyoto protocol, brought Australia through the GFC with hardly a bump, brought Australia into the prestigious G20 group of countries, declared climate change 'the greatest moral challenge of our time' promising stern measures to combat it, and implemented a home insulation scheme. Unfortunately, the latter was spoilt by some cowboy contractors, for which Rudd unfairly received the blame.

In short, Rudd was appearing as a resounding success as PM, although by 2010 public support declined over several mishaps: the mining super-profits tax was bungled, carbon pricing had been delayed, and his humane policies on asylum seekers saw a sharp rise in boat arrivals. Nevertheless, his ratings at that time were not as low as Howard's had been in his first term or Keating's in 1993, yet both were re-elected. To replace a PM who had been elected as PM, with someone who had not been elected as PM, was seen by many as an outrage. But that was to occur twice on the other side of the floor very few years later.

McKew's version of the reason for the ambush, quoting a Labor MP, was that 'Rudd treated some of the factional operatives like shit, which is to his eternal credit. He wasn't going to let them run his government and nor should he. He was contemptuous of them. They thought, we'll show you. And they did.' In McKew's words, Rudd 'didn't genuflect and kiss the ring' of the small group who saw themselves as the owners of the Labor Party.

Gillard's story

Gillard's *My Story*, written after the 2013 elections when she had left Parliament, tells her version of events, which is rather different from McKew's. The book is in two sections: How I did it, which is all about her tactics in deposing Rudd, and Why I did it, which outlines her beliefs and values and her views on various policies. The how and the why should be logically interrelated and it is perhaps typical of her that she keeps them separate: she sees herself in section 2 holistically as a person who perceives the wood, but section 1 is all about the trees. So who is 'the real Julia', the tactician or the policy strategist? The pragmatic 'why' – why she stood against Rudd – is not about policy but about the fact that, as she and others saw it, governance under Rudd was chaotic. As she said, 'the closer you were to the centre of the Rudd Labor Government the more critical you were of Kevin'.

Gillard says that Rudd did indeed treat his colleagues like shit, right from the start: summoning MPs to his office and making them wait often for hours, cancelling appointments well into their wait, ferocious temper tantrums that sometimes reduced female and male colleagues alike to tears, convening committees then overriding their recommendations, making spur of the moment headlines that threw plans into chaos. What concerned Gillard and colleagues even more was that when the UN Framework Convention on Climate Change (UNFCCC) Conference in Copenhagen had folded in disagreement – which the ever-diplomatic Rudd said had been 'rat-fucked by China' – Rudd had slipped into a mental state that made him incapable of leading the government. 'It was my strong belief,' she wrote, 'that after some recovery time, his (KR's) dominant emotion would be relief – he had become so wretched as leader.' In other words, 'I can see you are unhappy in your job, so I'll take your job away from you. I'm sure you will be relieved and even thank me!' He was not relieved, as his later behaviour showed. And he didn't thank her.

Gillard said that in January 2010 she tried to get Rudd to decide when to call an election and to start implementing his policies, particularly those on climate change, but he became increasingly impossible to deal with. And that, she and several colleagues decided by June, was no way to run the country. He had to be replaced, they decided, especially with an election looming. Which, as it turned out, was precisely the wrong decision.

Action on climate change

A major difference between McKew's and Gillard's accounts is about climate change. Gillard says she was always persuaded by the science on climate change and was strongly in favour of taking measures against it. She recalls that that had been Labor policy since both Hawke and Keating governments signed on to the UN convention on climate change, ratifying it in 1993, which led in turn to the Kyoto Protocol. Howard initially signed the protocol but negotiated massive reductions for Australia and later refused to ratify it.

Al Gore's *An Inconvenient Truth* made climate change a popular issue that forced Howard's hand and by 2007 both Labor and Liberals promised to create a market-based Emissions Trading Scheme (ETS). By 2008, however, public interest had cooled off due to several factors: the cost of carbon reduction, the (incorrect) assumption that electricity bills would soar, the GFC, the failure of the Copenhagen conference, questioning the science by some rogue nonclimate scientists and by out-and-out charlatans like Lord Monckton who didn't even have a science degree. All of this got massive media coverage, particularly in the Murdoch press. Tony Abbott, who also hadn't got a science degree, proclaimed authoritatively that 'the argument behind climate change is absolute crap'.

Although Rudd reacted badly to this change in public concern, a Carbon Pollution Reduction Scheme (CPRS) had been worked out by

December 2008, targeting 15% below 2000 emissions by 2020. Penny Wong, Wayne Swan and Rudd were a subcommittee to work out strategy on this basis but Rudd changed meeting dates on a whim, and progress was slow. Rudd then decided to postpone implementation by a year to allow business to recover from the GFC, but increasing the target to 25% by 2020 in order to assuage environmentalists. Rudd had thought he could take the CPRS to the December 2009 Copenhagen conference to show how Australia was leading the world. Unfortunately, the CPRS was defeated in the Senate in August, the Greens astonishingly siding with Liberals. The Greens had made a bad tactical mistake: had they voted with Labor, a carbon reduction scheme would have been in place for over nine years by now.

Malcolm Turnbull, then Opposition leader, and Rudd were negotiating a bipartisan deal – and that was why the hard right in the Liberal Party in 2009 saw Turnbull defeated as leader, if only by one vote. That was the end of any bipartisanship on action against climate change. The Coalition as Gillard says 'went from divided but mostly rational on carbon pricing, to united and irrational almost overnight'.

A report in the *Sydney Morning Herald* by Peter Hartcher gained immediate traction: that 'Gillard was determined to stop Rudd proceeding with the scheme'. Gillard said this was quite wrong. 'The suggestion that he was too weak to stand up to me if he wanted to is absurd.' Hartcher's report, undoubtedly sourced from Rudd, and the confusion between a tax and a trading scheme, led to a widespread belief that Gillard had used climate change action in an unprincipled and opportunistic way: for action in the 2007 election, against action in order to discredit Rudd, and for action again when doing a deal with the Greens. In her own account, however, she was consistent throughout and she and colleagues were thwarted by Rudd's dilly-dallying.

After Copenhagen, Rudd had wanted to move to a direct action scheme like Abbott's. Gillard and Penny Wong tried to dissuade him as it was 'obviously policy nonsense'. During 2010, Rudd was not campaigning any more on carbon reduction, whereas Abbott was kicking goals with his own strident messages. Gillard proposed post-poning legislation until a bipartisan agreement could be formed, which seems naïve given that the Opposition's hard-line policy was up and running. Worse, a cabinet leak said that the CPRS was to be taken out of the budget and was effectively off the agenda. All of this, a product of bad luck and bad management, did severe damage to Labor's credibility on climate change.

Gillard's account of action on climate change sees non-action as mostly Rudd's fault. McKew, on the other hand, makes no bones about what she sees as Gillard's position: 'Gillard wanted plans for an emissions trading scheme junked and from the beginning of 2010 never let up in putting forward this point… She thought the government should drop the whole idea of an ETS because it had become electoral poison. She told Rudd that under no circumstance would she support the case for an election based on the need for action on climate change.'

Who to believe?

Gillard's account might be read as overly defensive but on the other hand McKew could not have been present at most of these discussions, so she would not know for certain who had said what. If her source was Rudd or his 'cavaliers', then that's what they would say about Gillard. Both are probably partially correct. Gillard was ultimately for post-poning the Carbon Pollution Reduction Scheme (CPRS), which could be interpreted as her seeing it as electoral poison at the time when Abbott was storming on about 'this toxic tax'.

Gillard's performance re climate change was probably due more to poor management, on both her part and especially Rudd's, than to cynical opportunism on her part. Her 'there will be no carbon tax under the government I lead' and then passing the CPRS was a bad look, earning her the title of liar. But she didn't lie: the CPRS is not a tax. A carbon tax implies that the government would simply tax companies for their carbon emissions. The CPRS is an emissions trading scheme on permits that may be bought and sold at a fixed price. She should have pointed this out. Instead, she accepted Abbott's calling the CPRS a 'tax', even using the term herself. Years later, she admitted to that mistake. And in 2017 Abbott's former chief of staff Peta Credlin cynically admitted that Labor's climate change policy was never a carbon tax, but 'a label for brutal retail politics'.

Was Gillard planning or, as McKew would say, plotting against Rudd before the fateful 24 June 2010? Gillard says, 'I made a decision to run for Prime Minister on the day I walked into Kevin Rudd's office and I asked him for a ballot.' McKew does not believe this or that she was pushed into the PM's job at the last minute and against her will: 'Gillard's forensic attention to detail sets her apart and her careful planning of every career move is legendary.'

I tend to agree with McKew in doubting that Gillard was reluctantly pushed into the role of prime minister. She might have been reluctant about the timing – her preference would have been after the 2010 election – but things seemed so bad to some Labor ministers they acted before the election. That was another bad mistake. Had he remained leader, Rudd almost certainly would have delivered a majority Labor government in the 2010 election. And then, if he still behaved erratically after the election, he could have been replaced without much drama at all.

Gillard blames Rudd for the disaster of the mining super-profits tax. McKew claims it was Swan and the Treasury who so misjudged the timing and form of that tax. Swan in particular ignited the mining industry's expensive and effective thrust-back, when previously they and the government had agreed in principle to a different form of profits tax.

In reviewing McKew's and Gillard's stories, it is notable that the two did not like each other from the start. McKew was posted as parliamentary secretary for early childhood education (ECE) under Gillard, who was then Minister of Education. According to McKew, Gillard was condescending, authoritarian and didn't consult, and when McKew offered advice on ECE, which was her remit and a subject dear to her heart, Gillard ignored it. Despite all that, McKew together with the state education ministers stitched together a national framework for ECE and new professional standards for early childhood teachers.

Gillard for her part damns McKew with faint praise. Whereas McKew was proud of her achievement in brokering a national framework for ECE, Gillard wrote that 'Maxine had misread generalised support for change as specific support for a particular change.' When McKew lost Bennelong in 2010, Gillard commented, 'Maxine had found it hard to adjust from the adrenaline of the 2007 national- spotlight campaign to the day-to-day slog of being a marginal seat member.'

This is not at all how Maxine herself described her 2010 campaign.

Gillard as prime minister

McKew doesn't say much about Gillard's term as prime minister. In discussing the change of leadership, however, one must evaluate Gillard's performance. It is clear even from her own account that many things went wrong as she admits: timing, not least over ousting Rudd, asylum seeker policy and dithering about the mining tax and climate change policy. Neither did the silly egocentricity of 'the real Julia', and the vacuous 'moving forward', go down well.

All that said, however, her achievements were in fact considerable. She negotiated a minority government that survived the full term despite relentless attacks from the Opposition and the press, which says a lot for her negotiating skills. Her government passed important legislation, such as the CPRS, the national disability scheme, the mining tax, the Gonski education reforms and unfairness in superannuation tax. The performance of her government was also better than the Howard government's on inflation, interest rates, household savings, personal tax rate, company tax rate, international credit ratings, foreign exchange reserves, current account as a percentage of GDP, and balance of trade. It was a successful government by any standards.

This legislative history in one term in minority government is more than Howard was able to do in four terms with majority government.

Despite the appearance of mayhem, Gillard steered more positive legislation through parliament than had been passed under any other recent Australian prime minister.

Unfortunately, her government wasn't perceived to be successful, thanks to the lies and vicious attacks by the Opposition, all echoed in the Murdoch press. Almost equally important, her ministers didn't explain their policies. Rudd had real problems with the 'programmatic specificity' needed for adequate communication. He was continually trying to undermine Gillard. Both Swan and Gillard spoke in a way that invited people to switch off; and the distraction and hectic pace of the leadership change had placed a heavy workload on ministers. Whatever the reasons, the lack of adequate communication with the public was a grave mistake. They should have had, and deserved to have had, better PR about their work.

The vicious, personal and unprincipled attacks by the Coalition, and by Tony Abbott in particular, with the support of the Murdoch press, had misled the public. These attacks were all the more effective because of her lacklustre delivery – except for one memorable parliamentary speech in which she flayed Tony Abbott raw for his misogyny. Why didn't you treat us to more of that real Julia, Julia?

Climate change policy earned Gillard the sobriquet 'Juliar', jaw dropping in its hypocrisy coming from the likes of Tony Abbott. She notes that Keating and Howard changed their policies pre- and post-election many times but they were never branded John-liar or Pauliar. Likewise, Keating wasn't called a traitor for challenging Hawke, but she was for challenging Rudd. She believes, certainly correctly, that this was because women aren't supposed to challenge alpha males. She describes other sexist attacks on her in detail and they make sickening reading. She was rightly enraged but she handled the attacks with dignity, culminating in her powerful misogyny speech.

In her book, Gillard repeatedly says things like 'I drew on my resolve', 'The same sense of purpose to drive me on' and the like, which might give the picture of a strong determined person – but I'd rather she hadn't felt the need to keep telling us so. Show, don't tell: much more convincing.

Had the ALP become dysfunctional under Rudd II?

Internal fighting between pro- and anti-Rudd forces within Labor gave the public impression of a party and a government that was out of control. During the 2013 election campaign, the Coalition did not put up any positive policies beyond mindless three-word slogans such as 'stop the boats' and 'axe the tax', promising to dismantle virtually everything Labor had put up, and to bring the budget back to surplus without saying how. All that notwithstanding, Abbott easily and undeservedly won the 2013 election. That's how low Labor had been painted in public esteem by the press and Liberal name-calling.

No surprise then that McKew raises the wider issue of the functionality of the Labor party itself. There is the question of party discipline, of not speaking beyond instructions from above, of doing what you are told by brash unelected minders who think it appropriate to loudly abuse elected members at six in the morning, of having no part in discussing ideas even in the area of your remit and supposed expertise. And you'd better come from the traditional Labor background and have allegiance to one faction or another.

Given McKew's account, there seemed to be little hope for the ALP. It had lost its roots and had become a principle-free zone driven by spin and polling. The elected senior politicians governing the country were so craven, and/or so easily manipulated, that they did not speak out against what they later admitted to be patently wrong: deposing a popular leader in his first term as prime minister. The culture McKew describes is one of disrespect, bullying, game-playing and big-noting yourself if you want to survive. How can you represent your electorate when so hog-tied? This is not representative democracy or even any sort of democracy, for once elected you become the creature of an unelected minority, the factional powerbrokers.

A major problem for Labor is that since Hawke and Keating took neoliberal economic policy on board, the gap between Labor and Liberal narrowed drastically. To win against the Liberals, they had to outdo the Liberal Party on that party's own home ground, which also came to include what to do about asylum seekers and that it had better be very nasty. If policy is not differentiating the parties any more, personalities and presidential type leadership become paramount, as became very clear in the 2019 election. Significantly, Lindsay Tanner quit Parliament soon after Rudd's removal – not, he assured us, because he was on one side or the other on that issue, but because he was deeply disillusioned about them all. As he made clear in *Sideshow*, politics as amplified by an unprincipled press becomes all about spin and entertainment, not about governing the country well. And what more entertaining than the press reports of Rudd undermining Gillard.

After the 2010 election, Gillard said that Rudd 'brought all his formidable skills to bring me down and seize the leadership', but 'I was never going to voluntarily submit to the Labor Party being taken over by Kevin and those who had behaved so disgracefully…to do so seemed to me a tacit endorsement that their tactics were acceptable…to do so would be to signal that the Labor Party was no longer a party of purpose.' Really? Maxine's experience was hardly that of 'a party of purpose'.

When the party had already sacked Rudd for being unmanageable, unpredictable and finally incapable of action, to put him back into the leadership was unfathomably stupid. And he acted true to form, particularly in the last week of the 2013 election campaign when he proposed moving Sydney's naval facilities to Brisbane, and despite his previous 'humanitarian' stance on asylum seeker policy in his second term he tried to out-cruel the Coalition with his New Guinea solution of Manus Island, which turned out to be a terrible disaster. Replacing Gillard with the man they had previously found to be a chaotic leader, and under Gillard a treacherous wildcard, showed that the Labor Party was indeed no longer a party of purpose or of principle. They didn't seem to know where they were going.

Yet only three years later, it wasn't Labor that was sinking deeper and deeper into the mire but the Coalition. Parachuting the seemingly charismatic Malcolm Turnbull in to save the day didn't work. The bargain was that if he wanted to stay as leader, despite his previous middle-of-the-road views on climate change and same-sex marriage, he had to support his predecessor Abbott's policies. That bargain turned him into a hollow man. He caved in to the right to save himself only to lose everything (see Chapter 4).

Equally amazing was that Bill Shorten, who was instrumental in deposing both Rudd and then Gillard, at last provided the party with policies that differentiated Labor from the Coalition. Labor under Rudd and Gillard had bungled their head start on climate change, but under Shorten there was a turn-around: a commitment to 50% renewables by 2030, closure of coal-fired power stations and $500 billion to revitalise the Great Barrier Reef, to name a few.

However, the 2019 election scuppered Labor's apparent renaissance and at the time of writing it's back to the drawing board (see Chapter 6).

Books referred to

Gillard, Julia, *My Story*, Knopf, 2014.
McKew, Maxine, *Tales from the Political Trenches*, Melbourne University Press, 2012.
Tanner, Lindsay, *Sideshow: Dumbing down Democracy*, Scribe, 2011.

3

Was the Abbott Government Fascist?

After Tony Abbott had won the 2013 Federal election, and particularly after his broken promises and the 2014 budget, people were shocked at where Australia seemed to be heading. So where was Australia heading? Towards fascism? There were straws in the wind.

The Collins Dictionary defines fascism thus: n 1 any doctrine, system or practice regarded as authoritarian, militaristic, chauvinistic or extremely right-wing. That's something of a catch-all. There are several definitions which in common suggest that a fascist government has the following characteristics: a strong leader or small group of leaders with psychopathic tendencies; a culture of lying; it rules by fiat and slogan; has a culture of lying; defines and maintains an underclass while redistributing wealth and power to an elite; it filters information so that the government only receives advice it wants to hear; it controls the media; it is nationalistic and militaristic; it is a poor world neighbour; it takes over industry and commerce; and the strongest defining characteristic, it proposes to establish through violence a new ultra- nationalistic order.

How did the Abbott government stack up against these criteria?

A strong leader or small group of leaders with psychopathic tendencies

A fascist leader is obsessed with power and control for its own sake and will do whatever it takes to grab and maintain power. This suggests a strong streak of psychopathy. Psychologist Lyn Bender asks, 'What if Abbott and his cronies are just a bunch of psychopaths?'[21] Psychopaths are commonly described as lacking empathy and compassion, they do not reflect on their own behaviour, are narcissistic, do not experience guilt or remorse, are given to compulsive lying, seek revenge, and see the end as justifying the means. Bender made a startling case that Abbott and some of his ministers exhibited psychopathic tendencies, mentioning Joe Hockey and Scott Morrison, to whom one might now add Peter Dutton. Donald Trump shows all these characteristics in spades.

Abbott himself lacked empathy and compassion on several occasions. In October 2007, he accused dying asbestos victim Bernie Banton's public protest against James Hardy as 'a stunt'. During a visit to Afghanistan in February 2011, his comment on being told the details of how an Australian soldier had died was 'shit happens'. When a Channel 7 reporter questioned Abbott on this comment, he glared at the reporter, jerking his head for a full twenty-eight seconds, remaining silent, as if too outraged to trust himself to speak.[22] Later, on talkback radio, a grandmother on complaining about the budget said she was forced to do telephone sex work to make ends meet. Abbott smirked and gave the radio host a sleazy wink.

Laurie Oakes said these and other 'flat-footed comments will surely call his leadership of the Liberal Party into question…and he will pay dearly for it'. Oakes was correct, sooner than he had thought.

Rules by fiat and slogan

The following is attributed to Nazi leader Joseph Goebbels:

> The most brilliant propagandist technique will yield no success unless one fundamental principle is borne in mind constantly – it must confine itself to a few points and repeat them over and over.[23]

That was exactly how Abbott had conducted his campaign, with slogans such as 'stop the boats', 'repeal the carbon tax', 'earn or learn', repeated ad nauseam. No explanation, no justification. It worked for Goebbels, it worked for Abbott in the 2013 election, and it worked for Morrison in the 2019 election.

Political debate in a democracy has parties standing on different platforms. The idea is that come election time politicians argue their case with evidence and logic, taking apart their opponents' case likewise with evidence and logic. When candidates hurl insults at each other, as happens, they are the exhaust pollution that comes from a working engine. Before and during the last federal election, however, Tony Abbott brought political debate to an all-time low in Australia: the pollution of insults occurred without the working engine. And continued over the next two governments.

A culture of lying

Fascist governments survive through a culture of lying. Joseph Goebbels again:

> If you tell a lie big enough and keep repeating it, people will eventually come to believe it. The lie can be maintained only for such time as the State can shield the people from the political, economic and/or military consequences of the lie. It thus becomes vitally important for the State to use all of its powers to repress dissent, for the truth is the mortal enemy of the lie, and thus by extension, the truth is the greatest enemy of the State.[24]

Political lying is not defined in terms of broken promises, which happens in all parties, but as Alan Austin puts it, 'a knowingly false statement by a politician, expressed with the intention to deceive'.[25] On this criterion, Austin counted the lie score of recent political leaders as follows: Kevin Rudd 1, Alexander Downer 7, John Howard 15+, Tony Abbott 30, other recent leaders of all parties, including Julia Gillard, 0. The federal Liberals in the Abbott government were thus by far the most mendacious of all parties, and Abbott worse than other Liberals. In an interview with Abbott, Kerry O'Brien tried hard to pin Abbott down on about his lying.[26] Abbott's reply was essentially this: 'If I didn't put it in writing, more fool you for believing me.'

That poll, however, was taken before Scott Morison became leader. The Coalition penchant for lying was a tradition that Morrison worked into a fine art, as we see in Chapter 5.

Defines and maintains an underclass while redistributing wealth and power to an elite

Abbott destroyed virtually every positive initiative established by Labor: their social justice initiatives including Gonski, the National Disability Insurance Scheme, anything to do with combatting climate change, mitigating gambling reforms, superannuation tax relief for low income earners, and much more. Fortunately, the Senate blocked this assault on the least privileged. Four years later, Turnbull diluted Gonski funding and the NDIS in a bid to de-Abbottise Coalition policy (see Chapter 4).

In 2013, Australia had a Triple-A credit rating, twenty-two years free of recession, a strong health care system, and one of the lowest debt to GDP ratios in OECD countries. Yet the Abbott government claimed that in view of Australia's economic crisis (a lie), a really tough budget was necessary (another lie), and that ordinary Australians would have to do the 'heavy lifting' (yet another lie). The gaming industry had of course to be protected against proposed gambling reforms, so they were scrapped. All these changes would benefit the wealthy enormously and correspondingly hit the poor. In 2017–18, ABS figures showed that the wealthiest 20% of the population owned 60% of household net worth, while the lowest 20% owned less than 1%.

Abbott's 2014 budget pulled out all the neoliberal stops: it would have cut the school student bonus, but a paid parental leave scheme would hand up to $75,000 pa to already wealthy people. The super payments of those on $35,000 pa or less, previously tax free, would be taxed at 15%, while scrapping Labor's plan to tax the richest retirees' super funds handed a total of $300 million to the richest Australians. Taxes for small businesses would be increased but taxes (including the diesel tax) for mining and for corporations paying the carbon tax would be cut. And with a nasty placement of the boot, he would cut supplementary allowances for the unemployed on Newstart and youth allowances. Unemployed twenty-three-year-olds stood to lose 18% of their disposable income, an unemployed sole parent with an eight-year-old child would lose 12%. By contrast, a high-income couple with a combined income of $360,000 a year would lose nothing they'd notice. People under thirty would not receive any benefits at all if they lost their job, leaving them with nothing to live on. Family Tax Benefit would be restricted to those earning under $100,000 and payment stopped when their child reached six, previously sixteen. The 'heavy lifting' was to be done by those with the weakest arms.

The expenditure review committee preparing the 2014 budget, comprising Abbott, then-treasurer Joe Hockey and current Finance Minister Mathias Cormann, considered banning anyone under thirty years of age from accessing any income support, thereby saving $9 billion over four years. The idea was dropped as other members of the coalition thought the backlash would be too damaging. But it is an insight into the cruel way Abbott and company were thinking.

There was outrage when at budget time a lucky photo showed Treasurer Joe Hockey and Finance Minister Mathias Cormann sitting outside in the sun, enjoying fat cigars, grinning with self-satisfaction, presumably at the way in which they were proposing to shaft the lower orders.

Hockey advised the homeless that they could afford a house by 'getting a good job that pays good money'; he raged at those awful people who 'double-dipped' on a parental leave scheme or by earning a few bob while on welfare or studentships. When Turnbull as the incoming PM didn't appoint Hockey his Treasurer, as Hockey thought he deserved, he resigned from Parliament only to be rewarded for his incompetence by being made ambassador to the US at a salary of $360,000. In addition, he would receive his parliamentary pension of $90,000. Even then, when in New York, he charged his babysitting fees to us taxpayers back in Australia.

Double-dipping, Joe? You said that that was not nice when single mothers did it.

Policies on health and education

Related to creating an underclass were the attacks on health and education. The Abbott government would have introduced a $7 co-payment and increased pharmaceutical fees in the health budget as the first step in dismantling Medicare and setting up a more privatised health system along US lines. Note: the US spends 17.7% of GDP on health for a far worse and inequitable system than ours, whereas Australia spends 9.5% on health, including Medicare, for a much superior health service. This difference is largely attributable to the fact that if people don't go to the doctor, the later consequences can be expensive. The proposed budget intervention on health could not therefore have been about economics or efficiency of service; instead it looked like another deliberate hit at the poor.

The National Curriculum, started in 2008, lists a number of 'general capabilities', such as creative and critical thinking, ethical and intercultural understanding, that are likely to educate the public in critically evaluating government policy rationally. Education Minister Christopher Pyne described that curriculum as having a left-leaning bias, so he appointed two reviewers to ensure the curriculum is 'balanced and fair'. To ensure 'balance', one appointee was a Liberal Party staffer, the other ran a conservative think tank on educational issues. Both supported compulsory religious education in schools. The way of reason evidently has no place in a neoliberal education.

Abbott gutted the Gonski educational reforms with its egalitarian intent, but handed more largesse to independent schools; $245 million were allocated to finance untrained chaplains to provide ideologically tainted support for students, at the cost of many professionally trained social workers and psychologists. Abbott attacked science, research and education as if they were social vices; all the instrumentalities set up by Labor for climate change and renewable energy were abolished, except for Gillard's Clean Energy Finance Corporation, because the Senate stopped that one.

But there was meaning in all this madness. Fascist governments need an elite and an underclass. That is exactly what the budget and other legislation would have helped to define.

Filters information, controls the media

A fascist government does not want to entertain information or to consider possibilities it doesn't want to hear: 'the truth is the enemy of the State', as Goebbels had said.

Abbott stacked all committees and inquiries he set up with far-right-wingers and climate change deniers, such as the Royal Commission into pink batts and the National Commission of Audit. Clearly, he was interested not in seeking the truth but in gaining the result he wanted. Three years later, Donald Trump showed us how that really should be done.

SBS and especially the ABC were accused of left-wing bias, although most ABC current affairs panels like *The Drum* and *Q&A* carefully balance left- and right-wing invitees. Both SBS and ABC suffered heavy cuts after being promised pre-election there would be no cuts.

A fascist government controls the media, no dissent allowed. There was little need to filter the press for News Corp, which backs the far right 100% and is the most widely read.

Robert Manne wrote,

Murdoch's domination of the metropolitan press has two main consequences for our democracy. First, any government, no matter how worthy or unworthy, is now vulnerable should News Corp decide to target it in the way it targeted the Gillard government more than two years ago. Second, while News Corp retains its present dominance, mainstream debate about certain fundamental ideologically sensitive questions – how to respond adequately to the climate-change crisis; what levels and kinds of taxation are needed to develop the welfare state; the trajectory of foreign policy during the rise of China; Australia's Middle Eastern policy; and, of course, media reform – is effectively ruled out in advance.[27]

Then, if you throw in Ray Hadley, Andrew Bolt, Alan Jones and *Sky News*, all of which are on the far right and populist, you have a solid wall of right-wing propaganda in most of the media in Australia.

Is nationalistic and militaristic

The militarisation of Operation Sovereign Borders was entirely unnecessary, turning what should have been a humane rescue operation into a military exercise complete with military-style uniforms and tight security clamps on information. Its handling probably reflected Scott Morrison's militaristic fantasies as much as Abbott's, and later ex-cop Peter Dutton's. General Jim Molan, who controversially led US forces in attacking villages in Iraq, was appointed in charge of Operation Sovereign Borders with its militaristic stamp. He renamed it the Australian Border Force, kitting it out with its very own smart new uniform to make it look even more militaristic.

In that time of supposed financial crisis, defence spending was increased to $122.7 billion for the four years to 2018, which amounts to 2% of GDP, including the purchase of fifty-eight Lockheed Martin F-35 joint strike fighters for $12 billion. In military circles, even by Trump himself, the F-35 is regarded as a lemon: overpriced, too slow, lacking manoeuvrability and highly visible to radar. Oddly, the F-35 is designed for attack not for defence. Arming for defence makes sense for Australia, but who are we going to attack? Then there is a further $50 billion for twelve new submarines. A couple perhaps, but why twelve? It doesn't make clear sense in real world priorities for Australia.

Is a poor world neighbour

Being a good world neighbour means signing human rights treaties and adhering to them, and to international law. Australia has signed twelve such, including treaties on refugees, torture, rights of children and of people with disabilities. Many of these treaties have been broken with regard to Aborigines, as revealed in John Pilger's 2014 film *Utopia*, and in past and current asylum seeker policy.

Very damaging to our international reputation was an $8 billion cut in foreign aid to impoverished countries, lowering foreign aid currently to .23% of GDP, compared to England's .7%. Twenty% of all the cuts in foreign aid has been borne by the poorest countries in the world.

Abbott damaged foreign relations with Indonesia, with China, and with East Timor, the latter by defrauding Timor Leste of oil rights in favour of Woodside Petroleum's interests in oil, and a large gas deposit that ordinarily would lie in Timor-Leste's waters. Alexander Downer, Foreign Affairs Minister with a business connection with Woodside, ordered ASIS to spy on East Timorese negotiators. ASIS installed listening devices in the East Timorese government offices under the false premise of providing a foreign aid program. The ASIS man who blew the whistle, Witness K, and his lawyer Bernard Collaery revealed the criminal activities of the Australian government. Our bullying of East Timor was claimed to be 'in the national interest', when it was entirely in the interests of the Australian corporate giant Woodside Petroleum. Collaery and Witness K were charged in 2018 with breaching national security when it was essentially a commercial squabble over boundaries. Finally, in 2019, the boundaries were redrawn with UN intervention favouring Timor-Leste – but the charges against Collaery and Witness K still stand.

Abbott also managed to incur Indonesia's wrath by hacking into the private phones of the president, his wife and his close staff, and by invoking policies on asylum seekers that involved Indonesian support without checking first with Indonesia. For all of which he refused to apologise. Abbott's Australia did not make a very good global citizen.

The Minister for Immigration was given responsibility for border protection, which Scott Morrison (who in his youth must have been the meanest bully in the school playground) enthusiastically enacted. As mentioned, Morrison had militarised asylum seeker policy and, no questions answered, this was not the business of prying citizens. Some detainees were imprisoned indefinitely, including children, in order to discourage others from trying their luck. In his maiden speech to Parliament in 2008, Morrison said, 'From my faith I derive the values of loving kindness, justice and righteousness, to act with compassion and kindness, acknowledging our common humanity and to consider the welfare of others…' We'll try to square that circle in Chapter 5.

When Morrison later became Treasurer, he was replaced by ex-cop Peter Dutton, who turned out to be even nastier in his treatment of asylum seekers than Morrison. And weirdly for neoliberals, all this was achieved at much greater expense than processing them onshore, as had been done in the not so distant past. Clearly, populist tactics override neoliberal penny-pinching. Each asylum seeker on Manus and Nauru cost $1,600 per day, which is more than if they were housed in top-grade hotels in Sydney

The treatment of asylum seekers during and subsequent to the Abbott regime, breaks several signed treaties: separating children from parents, keeping legal asylum seekers in ignorance of when their claims will be processed, the foul and dehumanising conditions in the offshore detention centres under conditions that have already been judged by the UN and Amnesty International as comprising torture. Abbott disbanded the Immigration Health Advisory Group, the only body to give independent advice on the physical and mental health of asylum seekers. It was made illegal for any ex staff to comment on conditions in the camps or on the health of the inmates. What information did come through was shocking. However, Abbott did not oversee the worst cruelties on Nauru and Manus: that was to be Turnbull's and, later, Morrison's privilege.

In order to 'stop the boats', the government had to make coming by boat (but not by plane) nastier than the nastiness from which asylum seekers were fleeing. When boats of hopeful disbelievers in Australia's nastiness kept coming, Abbott and Scott Morrison resorted to extraordinarily silly expediencies: buying Indonesian fishing boats in Indonesia so that none would be available to come to Australia; towing the people-smuggling boats back into Indonesian waters; packing asylum seekers into lifeboats and sending them back to Indonesia. All violated Indonesian territory. Relations with our most important neighbour had been seriously damaged. Stopping the boats had Abbott praising Sri Lanka's murderous regime, presenting President Mahinda Rajapaksa with two patrol boats in order to help stop any Sri Lankan asylum seekers leaving for Australia. Such tactics severely undermined Australia's international reputation as a humane country.

Abbott's worst as a world neighbour was on climate change. Australia was then and still is per capita the largest carbon-emitting country in the world. We are obliged to do our global bit. Not according to Abbott or subsequent Coalition leaders. As we have seen, on gaining government in September 2013, Abbott's first priority was to repeal carbon pricing, debasing the issue from one about global climate change to one about electricity bills. He accused the Warsaw global summit on climate change of 'socialism masquerading as environmentalism'. Australia sabotaged the summit, doing much damage to Australia's already sinking international image.

Abbott's international image was not enhanced on John Oliver's hilarious *Last Week Tonight* show on Abbott's first visit to the US as Australian PM.[28]

Takes over industry and commerce

In fascist countries, the state owns or otherwise controls industry and the means of production. This is not so in Australia but rather the other way around: corporate power owns the government. The results for us ordinary folk, however, are much the same.

In Australia, in 2013 company tax rate is 30% but few pay that. The average rate is 22% for companies, but Westfield paid 8% in 2013, and through a loophole, Apple, Google, Chevron and many others pay virtually no tax at all despite enormous profits made in Australia. Labor tried to fix that but the Abbott government dumped the Labor initiative.

The mining tax on 2011 rates would now be yielding about $60 billion per annum but after a ferocious campaign by both mining corporations and the Liberal Opposition, PM Gillard watered it down so much it yielded nothing in the first year although it would have raised around $3.8 billion over four years. Finance Minister Mathias Cormann wanted to abolish it altogether, claiming through a convoluted flow-on argument that it would save $13.8 billion. The diesel fuel rebate cost the government $5.4 billion in 2012–13, which was 'fair', because Murdoch's *Australian* said so (10 May 2014).

As for the environment, Abbott's intentions were that the Great Barrier Reef be a dumping ground for the foreign-owned (and thus non-taxpaying) Carmichael mine, World Heritage nominations dropped, marine parks around Australia scrapped, the Tasmanian Forestry Agreement ripped up, the 'greatly endangered' listing of the Murray-Darling Basin removed, which with other factors led to a catastrophe in 2018 (see pp. 100–102). All environmental assessments for development projects were to be handed to the states, most of whom want the royalties from development whatever the environmental cost, as in Queensland, NSW, West Australia and Tasmania.

Proposes to establish through violence a new ultra-nationalistic order

Fascist governments take the country in a radical new direction. Abbott himself is ultra-nationalistic – but to which country, Britain or Australia? – and pre-election Abbott had promised no surprises, steady as she goes. Yet post-election we were taken in what many thought was indeed a radical new direction, in flat contradiction to many of Abbott's electoral promises.

However, he has never at any stage proposed overthrowing the established order to set up a new system. This is an extreme definition of fascism which fits Mussolini's Italy and Hitler's Germany, possibly Trump's America, but fortunately did not fit Abbott's Australia.

So was the Abbott government fascist?

When an earlier version of this chapter appeared on *Tasmanian Times* in June 2014, soon after that ill-judged 2014 budget, it attracted an unusually large number of comments (147). Some agreed that the Abbott government showed many signs of fascism, others that there were some signs but calling it 'fascist' was going too far. Others wrote that I wouldn't have been able to publish the article if Australia was really a fascist country. Point taken.

Hard line neoliberalism, which is largely but not only what the Abbott government was about, certainly has many of the characteristics of fascism.[29] But in the end the most telling characteristic of Abbott's term as PM was in the 'captain's calls' Abbott made, most of which were simply bizarre: his parental leave scheme for the very rich, the knighting of Prince Philip, appointing the unhinged partisan Bronwyn Bishop as Speaker of the House, ordering his ministers to boycott ABC's *Q&A*, the list is mind boggling. Evan Williams's *Australian Leader Eats Raw Onion Whole* (Black Inc., 2015) contains headlines inspired by Abbott's actions and some of his quotations, including the plain barmy 'loggers are the ultimate conservationists'.

The cover of Niki Savva's book *The Road to Ruin* says it all.[30] The subtitle – 'How Tony Abbott and Peta Credlin destroyed their own government' – and a revealing assessment on the cover by Laurie Oakes: '…the weirder-than-weird story of a duo who couldn't govern to save themselves'. And on the back cover: 'Abbott ignored all the warnings, from beginning to end – the public ones, the private ones, from his friends, his colleagues, the media.'

Abbott on the backbench

When Abbott lost the leadership to Turnbull, he said,

> My pledge today is to make this change as easy as I can. I've never leaked or backgrounded against anyone. And I certainly won't start now. This is a tough day, but when you join the game, you

accept the rules. Being the Prime Minister is not an end in itself; it is about the people you serve.

An admirable statesmanlike comment. As it turned out, he couldn't have meant a word of it. He skirmished, with that familiar leer, making statements on issues that backbenchers don't make but that wannabe-again PMs do. He lectured the British conservatives and Europe in general on how to manage their refugee problem – simple: make things worse for them than if they had remained in their own country. He assured his British audience he would be returning as PM of Australia.

He tried to undermine Turnbull's authority wherever he could, backed by a small cadre of extreme right Coalition members, including Eric Abetz, George Christensen, Craig ('renewable energy will kill people this winter') Kelly and others.

After the 2017 budget, Abbott charged the Coalition of being 'Labor-lite', warning that it risks a 'drift to defeat'. 'Why not say to the people of Australia: we'll cut the (Renewable Energy Target), to help with your power bills; we'll cut immigration, to make housing more affordable; we'll scrap the Human Rights Commission, to stop official bullying; we'll stop all new spending, to end ripping off our grandkids; and we'll reform the Senate to have government, not gridlock.' A singularly unpalatable list of non sequiturs.

He accused the government of losing direction and it needed his help to deal with the Senate crossbench. Abbott hardly got a thing through the Senate precisely because he couldn't or wouldn't negotiate with the cross bench.

Abbott was in younger days strongly influenced by Bob Santamaria. Santamaria was originally a major force in the Labor Party but with his strong Catholicism saw it as too soft on Communism, so he formed the Democratic Labor Party, which split Labor and kept it out of power for twenty-odd years. That sort of rigid Catholic dogmatism was the way Abbott worked and although he denied it, his policies were founded on a bedrock of hard Catholicism. A group of hard right Coalition politicians are also strong Catholics, including

Barnaby Joyce, Kevin Andrews, Andrew Robb, Joe Hockey and others. Just how these, and other self-professed Christians like Scott Morrison and Eric Abetz, can push policies that are diametrically opposed to Christ's teachings is another of those mystifying flights of unreason. Their 'Christianity' is manifested in their unique twist to the Magnificat: 'We have filled the rich with good things and the hungry we have sent empty away.' No doubt they sing the original version on Sundays.

However Abbott may rationalise that inconsistency, his behaviour after the leadership spill has been by any standards irrational, nasty and at that time likely to bring about the very thing he would most deplore, a Shorten government. Accordingly, he is regarded as a damned nuisance by many of his Liberal colleagues. He was showing no self-awareness or awareness of political reality. His speech to a group of climate deniers in London in October 2017 was plain crazy. He declared that climate change was a Green inspired fraud because more than a hundred years of photography at Manly Beach in his electorate did not show a rise in sea level; that bushfires were not worse than previously, droughts not deeper or longer, and cyclones not more severe than they were in the 1800s. 'It's climate change policy that's doing harm; climate change itself is probably doing good; or at least, more good than harm.' But – a bet another way – if however the climate *is* warming, then,

> as far more people die in cold snaps than in heatwaves, so a gradual lift in global temperatures, especially if it's accompanied by more prosperity and more capacity to adapt to change, might even be beneficial.

After Turnbull's benchmark for topping Abbott passed, thirty negative Newspolls, Abbott publicly wondered why Turnbull's benchmark applied to Abbott and not to himself. In a flurry of non sequiturs, Abbott led a group calling themselves the Monash Forum – to the anger of the descendants of Sir John Monash – comprising far right climate deniers such as Eric Abetz, Craig Kelly, Kevin Andrews,

Barnaby Joyce and others, all of whom have a deep grudge against Turnbull. Abbott rode his bike around the Latrobe Valley campaigning for a government-built new coal-fired power station, knowing full well that, at that time, it was contrary his government's energy policy. The only certain effect of this silliness would surely be to split the Coalition and thus to keep it out of power for the foreseeable future. It seemed that Abbott and his backers would rather cripple the Liberal Party than compromise their extreme minority views, and at the same time pull Turnbull from his prime ministerial perch. They toppled Turnbull but against all expectations the Coalition survived.

As Peter van Onselen wrote in the *Australian*,

> Team Abbott has two aims. The first is to wound Turnbull as regularly and substantially as possible. The second is to assume control of the wreckage left behind — the Coalition (and the Liberal Party within it) — once on the opposition benches. The required precursor is a hefty election defeat. It's akin to fighting over a stripped carcass, the way vultures and hyenas may do.[31]

Such irresponsible and ill-informed behaviour from a once Rhodes Scholar is more symptomatic of psychopathy or monumental ego-centrism than of fascism.

I'm happy therefore to conclude that Tony Abbott wasn't a true fascist. Rather, in his formative years he probably spent too much time taking a battering around the head in the boxing ring.

4

The Transmogrification of Malcolm Turnbull

A change but no change

Malcolm Turnbull's accession to the prime ministership on 14 September 2015 was greeted with a wave of euphoria, high expectations and profound relief. Two years of gross incompetence, mendacity, fear-mongering, confrontation and inhumane policies were finally over. Turnbull would, many believed, provide a sea change in Australia's political dynamics and direction.

Turnbull asserted he would foster discussion of issues, no shouting simple-minded three-word slogans. As he enthused to the Brisbane Club in an encouraging nine-word slogan, 'We're creative, we're innovative, and increasingly we think globally.' Parliament immediately seemed a happier workplace, and voters were more relaxed about politics. Turnbull looked and sounded like a statesman. We felt comfortable with having such a prime minister.

But we had also felt comfortable with Kevin Rudd's first accession to the prime ministership, with his fine rhetoric and promises of a new deal. But while Rudd delivered much of symbolic significance, he delivered little actual action. Instead, he went feral. It wasn't long before Turnbull too moved to the next phase in the Rudd-cycle: rhetoric but little action.

Indeed, from early on, Turnbull fumbled, beginning with his appointment and disappointment of ministers. Resources Minister Ian Macfarlane tried to join the Nationals but the Nats wouldn't have him: nor would the Liberals after that. Minister of Cities Jamie Briggs was sacked for sexually harassing a young staffer on a trip to Hong Kong then gallantly posting her image to his mates. Mal Brough was forced to resign over copying the Slipper diaries, Minister Stuart Robert for using a private trip to China to negotiate a deal between a mate of his and the Chinese government (an unrepentant Robert later re-emerged in fellow Pentecostal Scott Morrison's cabinet). Not a good start for Turnbull's government.

From May 2013 to September 2016, twenty-five state or federal parliamentarians had been forced to resign from their party or from the executive following allegations of misconduct. Twenty-two were from the Coalition, three from Labor, none from the Greens or independents.[32]

Turnbull invited a tax debate, but rather like Rudd when it came to the crunch, he was smitten with indecision. Three months to budget time, Turnbull started copying Labor's tax policies: Labor said no to raising the GST, Turnbull followed, overriding Treasurer Morrison, who wanted to raise the GST. Labor said let's limit negative gearing to new houses only, Turnbull immediately followed suit but a few days later, Turnbull bellowed that Labor's negative gearing policy would 'smash' the value of the family home. From everything being on the table for tax policy Turnbull gradually ruled out all alternatives, except cutting superannuation concessions for the very rich – and that outraged his extreme right, George Christensen threatening to cross the floor over it. Turnbull next proposed turning the clock back over seventy years by giving the states the right to levy income tax in order to pay for public education and for health; private schools, however, would continue to be lavished with federal money. The states rejected that idea in short order.

Parliament's sojourn in happy land was brief. The price Turnbull had to pay for his prime ministership was a Faustian agreement with the hard right of his party and there he remained throughout his prime ministership. It was the same old nasty politics, this time wrapped in a nice smile rather than a saurian leer.

Turnbull on asylum seekers

Turnbull continued offshore processing in Nauru and Manus Island and Abbott's policy of making conditions as bad or worse than those the refugees were fleeing from. When it emerged in the Cabinet Files fiasco in 2018 (see pages 82–83) that the Immigration Department had advised then Immigration Minister Morrison that up to 700 asylum seekers 'must' be granted permanent protection under existing legislation. Morrison instead asked ASIO to slow down security checks so deadlines would be missed, thus preventing some thirty extra asylum seekers a week from being granted protection. It also meant that refugees about to start a new, permanent life in Australia would only be allowed to stay for three years.

On being outed on this breach, Morrison offered an irrelevant defence: 'As minister for Immigration and Border Protection, it was my policy and practice to put Australia's national security interests first.' At which Prime Minister Turnbull sang his praises: 'Scott [Morrison] stopped the boats, he did an outstanding job in securing our borders.' Thereafter, the cry of 'national security' became a marvellous device for wedging Labor over much legislation such as silencing whistle-blowers and the press over issues that had nothing to do with national security and everything to do with saving governmental face.

In 2016, 267 refugees including eighty children and their families came to Australia from Nauru for medical treatment. A High Court challenge to the legality of detention on Nauru was dismissed, at which Turnbull intoned, 'The people smugglers will not prevail over our sovereignty… We must not give one skerrick of encouragement to people smugglers.' As if the issue was about people smugglers, not about how badly people who are legally seeking asylum are treated when they need medical treatment under Australia's duty of care.

In October 2016, Turnbull proposed a bill banning Nauru and Manus asylum seekers, once resettled as citizens of another country, from ever visiting Australia no matter the reason: family reunion, business, whatever. This was cruel, divisive, unnecessary and probably unenforceable.

In his phone conversation with Donald Trump about the deal Obama had made on resettling asylum seekers, Turnbull said, 'You can decide to take them or to not take them after vetting. You can decide to take 1,000 or 100 or none at all. It is entirely up to you.' Turnbull quite wrongly called the asylum seekers 'economic refugees', and he admitted they were Australia's responsibility. 'They have been under our supervision for over three years now and we know exactly everything about them.' But hadn't Turnbull assured UNHCR and the Australian people the conditions under which they were living were the responsibility of the governments of New Guinea and Nauru? In return, Turnbull agreed to accept a handful of US asylum seekers, two of whom were Rwandans who had cleared Australian security screening but who had already pleaded guilty to the murder of eight tourists. A nice deal. Turnbull was telling Trump quite a different story from that he had been telling the Australian people. During that call Trump asked a very good question: 'Why have you not let them into your society?' Why indeed.

In April 2016, the PNG Supreme Court ruled that detention on Manus was against the PNG constitution and that the 800 asylum seekers must go. But not to Australia, Peter Dutton swore. A year later they were still there – as unwilling residents. The locals physically attacked the refugees if they went into the neighbourhood so the refugees stayed in the camp. Australia built new quarters to which the asylum seekers were ordered to move but they refused; the quarters weren't finished, were unfurnished, and worse, they were unprotected from attacks by locals. Turnbull and Dutton simply denied the new quarters weren't finished or that they were unsafe. The refugees stayed in the old camp for a week without food, water and electricity before being forcibly moved.

The United Nations Human Rights Committee said these refugees were indeed Australia's responsibility and that Australia should close the camps immediately, taking 'all measures necessary to protect the rights of refugees and asylum seekers affected… Australia could not pick and choose which laws it followed and which rights it wanted to uphold.' But as Abbott had said, 'Australia was sick and tired of being lectured to by the UN.'

Peter Dutton was directly responsible for what many see as crimes against humanity. One example: the Somali refugee Abyan was raped and made pregnant while imprisoned on Nauru. She came to Australia for an abortion (illegal on Nauru) but Dutton claimed she refused it and was sent back five days later still pregnant. But she denied she had refused the abortion. The courts had said that refugees requiring medical treatment in Australia should not be returned to Manus and Nauru. An outraged Peter Dutton said this made 'passing policies difficult…this is ripping the system off.' He also complained that lawyers giving their time free to prevent the government from abusing refugees were 'un-Australian'. Dutton lied about refugees being attacked by locals, and about the vile conditions on Manus, asserting photographs and videos of squalid conditions were faked.

But he at least must have been having a good time, for he said of his job, 'I enjoy it a lot.'

What sort of person does that make him? An editorial in the *Saturday Review* (2 September 2017) answered that question thus:

There is nothing to see in Dutton except the worst of what this country could be. We can only be thankful that the court he so criticises stops him from taking us there with him. He plays politics as if it were a game but there is nothing to win, only losses.

Turnbull's opinion was startlingly different:

Peter Dutton is a thoughtful and committed and compassionate immigration minister… [He] is doing an outstanding job as immigration minister.[33]

Turnbull on climate change

Turnbull continued Abbott's Direct Action policy on climate change, widely regarded by climate scientists as expensive and ineffective. Turnbull himself had described Direct Action in 2011 as 'bullshit'. Yet he took this bullshit policy to the 2015–16 Paris Climate Change conference praising it to the skies. Turnbull derided Labor's 2020 climate change target promising 23% of energy to come from renewables as 'mad, a danger to the economy': only a few years earlier he had pushed for bipartisan action on climate change.

In February 2016, the Turnbull government established a new Growth Centre to drive innovation, competitiveness and productivity – but across the oil, gas, coal and uranium sectors. Not a cracker for renewable energy. He was clearly not going to repeat standing up for his beliefs as he had done in 2011. That is, assuming they were his beliefs.

In December 2016, Environment Minister Josh Frydenberg said that his department would look at an Emissions Intensity Scheme (EIS), which would allow lower carbon emitters to sell credits to higher emitters, effectively lowering the price of electricity. After yells of outrage from the right, Turnbull flatly denied that an EIS would be considered. The following day, Frydenberg denied that he had even used the words 'emissions intensity' (he had – it was on record). Turnbull reiterated: EIS or any form of carbon pricing would send household electricity bills soaring.

But the government's chief scientist, Alan Finkel, had reported positively on an EIS to the Council of Australian Governments (COAG), saying that an EIS was the most effective, greenest and cheapest option to reduce carbon emissions. He emphasised that an EIS would lower prices in the average household by $215 a year, saving $15 billion over 10 years.

Michelle Grattan commented,

…to refuse even to consider an EIS for the electricity sector –

which is a long way from a broad emissions trading scheme, or a carbon tax – is abject surrender, and a major failure of Turnbull's nerve and leadership… The bottom line is that the government's decree is absurd – a product of ideology (on the right), expediency (hey, let's score against Labor, which supports an EIS) and fear (Turnbull feeling the bounds of the not-so-gilded cage to which his party has consigned him).[34]

Finkel was ordered to produce another report more palatable to the climate change deniers. This second report aimed to reduce emissions in the electricity sector by 28% below 2005 levels by 2030, to introduce a Clean Energy Target between 2020 to 2030, to encourage new power plants to be built including renewable energy, gas, and coal with carbon capture and storage. He had put 'clean' coal back on the table. Finkel's second report is a political document designed to be acceptable to both Labor, who want carbon pricing and the Coalition who won't have a bar of it. Perhaps Finkel should have stuck to the hard science

In his determination to maintain coal-fired power, Turnbull requested AGL, the owners of the fading Liddell power station, to keep Liddell going for another five years. AGL refused, saying it was too expensive and they were repurposing it for clean energy. Here was the industry itself backing clean energy against coal and the government doing its best to boost coal.

Turnbull gave notice that his government would underwrite a loan of $1 billion to massively wealthy Indian company Adani for infrastructure to the Carmichael coal mine, the emissions from which would yield more than Australia's total carbon emissions. But that was all right, as one Liberal politician put it, because the coal is mostly to be sold to China and India and so the resulting emissions will not affect our carbon targets. A good point – but only if each country had its own impermeable pocket of airspace.

Adani's Carmichael mine requires dumping dredged sea floor within the Great Barrier Reef National Park when one-third of the

GBR had already been killed and the rest endangered; twelve billion litres of fresh water per annum would be taken from the Great Artesian Basin to the detriment of other users of that precious resource. Adani is noted in India for environmental vandalism and corruption.[35] Turnbull claimed it would produce 10,000 jobs, whereas Adani's own figure is 1,500.

In May 2017, Westpac joined other major banks in refusing to finance the Carmichael mine, to the fury of Nationals Senator Matt Canavan, who said Westpac had given in to 'a few extremists' (who comprised a majority of the population). Fortunately, Turnbull's 'loan' of $1 billion for a rail link required the Queensland government's approval. This was forthcoming at first but such was the public outrage, Premier Annastacia Palaszczuk withdrew it during her election campaign. However, Palaszczuk was spooked at the 2019 election result, in which Labor was annihilated in rural Queensland on the grounds it was ambivalent about coal mining, so Queensland Labor waved Adani through in a hurry, and on 13 June 2019 the last official hurdle was removed. The water licence granted to Adani puts no limit on the water it can take from the Great Artesian Basin. There will certainly be appeals, however, as there has not been a proper scientific analysis of the environmental damage it would certainly cause.

The Adani affair illustrates yet again not only Turnbull's terrible judgement, and his weakness in giving in to his bullying right-wing. Days before the opening of the 2019 election campaign, Environment Minister Melissa Price suddenly signed the final federal approval for Adani to proceed after being threatened with the sack by Nationals James McGrath if she didn't, despite the fact he hadn't the power to sack her.

The behaviour of all involved in the Adani scandal remained thoroughly opportunistic and short term, if not criminal, knowing as we do the complex and long-term effects of a mine that size would have.

Science for the chop

The head of the CSIRO, Larry Marshall, entrepreneur and venture capitalist appointed by Abbott, announced a cut of 330 jobs from the CSIRO. A hundred and ten jobs were from the CSIRO's Oceans and Atmosphere and Land and Water divisions, which were doing research crucial to climate change monitoring. Almost 3,000 scientists from more than sixty countries roundly condemned this attack that would 'decimate' its climate change research capabilities, warning the cuts would leave the Southern Hemisphere 'with no sustainable world-class climate modelling capability'. It was within Turnbull's power to bring Marshall back into line, even to sack him. Yet when Greg Hunt was moved from the Environment to be Minister of Science, he (not Turnbull) ordered the CSIRO to return to monitoring work on climate change, restoring $3.7 million and fifteen new jobs. But it was too little too late; 275 jobs were already gone, including Hobart's Dr John Church. The CSIRO's lead in climate science had been crippled.

China came to the rescue. In May 2017, a $20 million Centre for Southern Hemisphere Oceans Research (CSHOR), a joint venture between the CSIRO and China's Qingdao National Laboratory for Marine Science and Technology, was announced. Over five years, the Chinese will stump up $10 million and the CSIRO $8.25 million with the University of New South Wales, where Dr Church ended up, and the University of Tasmania adding the remainder.

Larry Marshall implausibly insisted this was not a backflip.

The 2016 double dissolution election

Turnbull's biggest political mistake was to call a double dissolution election on the ground that Senate had twice rejected a proposal to establish the Australian Building and Construction Commission (ABCC) in order to investigate corruption in the building industry. The election campaign was a long eight weeks, in which the ABCC itself was scarcely mentioned.

Turnbull's real aim in calling the election was to clear the Senate of independent and small party cross-benchers, who had got there in the 2013 election on the basis of tricky preference trading. He should have called a normal half Senate election for, as Turnbull should have well known, in a double dissolution election the margin for a seat is halved to 7.5%, making it that much easier for minor parties to get elected. And they did, including four One Nation seats. The Coalition's lower house previously comfortable majority was slashed to a very vulnerable one seat, while in the Senate Turnbull now had to win over nine out of eleven cross-benchers, including those four wild card One Nation senators.

'We have an economic plan' Turnbull kept assuring us with charm and authority, the field marshal rallying the troops. But that plan was to deliver massive tax cuts to the corporate world, up to $60 billion over ten years. That would deliver jobs and growth on an unheard-of scale! Neoliberal spin of course: we know that the trickle-down effect simply does not happen. What does happen is that under lower tax, companies make more profit, shareholders get a better dividend, Australian companies park their wealth in offshore tax havens as did Turnbull himself on the Cayman Islands, while the profits of the many foreign-owned companies disappear overseas mostly untaxed. The lower orders get sod all. It is well established that if you want to set the economy rolling, you don't channel big money to those who already have it, because they only reinvest it, whereas if the large majority of people have room to spend, they will and the economy responds. Scandinavian countries have known that for years. Kevin Rudd proved it by giving everyone money to spend to stave off the effects of the HFC and it worked.

Labor, on the other hand, performed better in the 2016 election than expected, coming within a whisker of winning. Bill Shorten had campaigned on funding education and health rather than the corporate sector, and he would reduce negative gearing to bring house prices down. What is astonishing is not that Turnbull won, if only by one seat, but that he was not thoroughly smashed. Who, except a corporate player, would in their right mind vote for Turnbull's bogus 'economic plan' over Shorten's backing health and education? Yet that flash of unreason occurred yet again in the 2019 election.

Had Turnbull gone to elections quickly when he was riding high, he would have won handsomely. And had he not gone for a double dissolution but a normal half-Senate election, Hanson herself would probably have been elected but not three more One Nations senators who were later to cause him big trouble. As Hanson had moved Howard's centre of gravity to the right, so she did Turnbull's, with the further complication that with only a one vote margin, any Coalition member could hold Turnbull to ransom by threatening to cross the floor. As one member did.

The Royal Commission into Banking

For years we had been shocked by malfeasance by the big four banks, offering mortgages to borrowers who couldn't repay, offering financial advice detrimental to the customer but to the advantage of the bank, unstated charges, unfair interest rates, and much more. Labor had been requesting a royal commission for years but Turnbull, an ex-banker himself, steadfastly refused. Instead, he invited the bank CEOs to have a cup of tea with him to sort things out. However, some of his National colleagues had constituents who had suffered severely at the hands of the banks, and insisted on a royal commission or they would cross the floor and vote with Labor and the Greens on the issue. Turnbull capitulated on 3 December 2017 only three days after having definitely ruled it out.

The banks themselves were not averse to a royal commission: a nice gentle one, say, to clear their public image. Turnbull announced the terms of reference that explained all. Superannuation was in the remit, including not-for-profit funds that over more than twenty years had consistently outperformed the funds run by the banks. Initially, there were no provisions for bank-wronged members of the public to make their submissions, which was what the whole thing was supposed to be about. The ACTU started gathering submissions, forcing the royal commission to invite the public in.

The Commissioner, Kenneth Hayne QC, however, soon showed he meant business, to the banks' joint consternation. We learned that the Commonwealth Bank and others generously took fees but offered no service, staff even forging customers' signatures – when the clients had died years previously. Already the Commonwealth has paid back $118 million to deceived customers but in June 2018 they were whacked with a $700 million fine, the largest in corporate history.

Insurance company AMP had actually falsified over twenty reports they had presented to the watchdog Australian Securities and Investment Commission (ASIC), not that ASIC would have done anything, having prosecuted only one court case in ten years. Rather it was the public outing and outrage that forced AMP's CEO, secretary and senior lawyer to resign. Other heads were to roll later, including once admired Ken Henry, chairman of NAB.

The findings of the royal commission have been described as revealing the worst scandal yet in Australian financial institutions. Turnbull, in his reluctance to have a royal commission enquiring into 'our most trusted institutions', had been completely discredited. He and other Liberals must have known what would be likely to come out in the event of a royal commission, but capitulated only when the Nationals threatened to cross the floor over the issue.

We might remind ourselves that Turnbull, a banker himself, has tax-free havens in the Cayman Islands.

LBGTI and gay marriage

The Safe School curriculum was intended to minimise bullying in schools, especially of lesbian, gay and transgender students. Safe Schools was implemented under the Abbott government, but once Turnbull was in charge, his rabid right demanded the curriculum be withdrawn, some claiming Safe Schools taught students to be homosexual. Senator Eric Abetz even argued that homosexuality was a lifestyle choice and that homosexuals could choose to be heterosexual if they wanted to.[36] These right-wingers demanded changes that would do the very thing the programme was designed to stop: focusing discrimination onto LGBTI students

There is a genetic component in determining homosexuality, which implies that disallowing a gay couple the right of marriage might well be the start of disallowing other rights to people with genetically determined factors. That places race in the equation, doesn't it, Eric?

Turnbull originally said that the gay marriage issue should be settled in Parliament, but his right extremists wanted a plebiscite, presumably as a delaying tactic. However, it later turned out to be more than that: a rallying call to the religious right to the conservative cause. Turnbull not only promised a plebiscite but added that it needn't be binding, which would make it a $160 million exercise in futility. But it didn't matter: Labor came out against any plebiscite, to the delight of both the right and of the LBGTI community itself. The right had been assured by Attorney-General George Brandis that they had every right to be bigots, while the LBGTI community for their part would rather delay a public debate and the harassment and bullying such a debate would create. They'd rather leave it until a decent parliamentary debate could occur if Labor obtained government.

In the event, the Senate twice rejected a plebiscite, so the government went to Plan B dreamt up by Peter Dutton: a voluntary postal ballot at a cost of $122 million, making this a cheaper exercise in futility than the plebiscite. The turnout for the last postal vote was 55%, the right no doubt hoping that it would be less for this vote. This turned out to be spectacularly wrong: the turnout was nearly 80%, and of this the yes vote was nearly 62%.

Turnbull had the gall to claim that his promise of a plebiscite had been kept by holding the postal vote, which is not a plebiscite. In a press conference, he said with his staged gravitas, 'Strong leaders carry out their promises. Weak leaders break them. I'm a strong leader.' At which Michelle Grattan commented, 'It was an unconvincing "Me Tarzan" moment.'[37]

The government had given the impression they were giving the voters a voice, while equally determined not to be bound by what the voters told them. This same strategy was repeated in the Aboriginal community's 'Uluru statement from the Heart': Turnbull sought Aboriginal opinion then ignored it.[38]

However, this time the postal vote result was so strong there was no question that the same-sex marriage bill would not be presented to Parliament, albeit with determined efforts by the right to weaken it with amendments to allow all kinds of dissent on religious grounds. The bill passed overwhelmingly, with four nos and nine abstentions. The announcement of the result set off an extraordinary scene of cheering and clapping. Turnbull with much strutting and crowing claimed the result as a major victory, as if it was all his doing. But hadn't he thrown up the obstacles the right had handballed to him: a plebiscite and a postal vote? He hadn't even campaigned for a yes vote, although he had always claimed to be in favour.

Labor had long argued that the same-sex marriage issue should be settled by a vote in Parliament. Shorten rightly said that the postal vote was a ridiculous waste of time and taxpayers' money, and that Turnbull would be 'responsible for every bit of the filth that debate will unleash'. The postal vote did stir up gay hate and suffering to children of gay couples as Shorten and many others had predicted it would. The yes vote finally succeeded but no thanks to Turnbull's weak leadership.

All Turnbull can claim on same-sex marriage is that he happened to be PM at the time. And that is all. If he had shown leadership on the issue, it would have passed Parliament months earlier with little of the nastiness that had been flung from the extremes on both sides.

Problems with the attorney-general

Turnbull had previously emphasised the important principle that public servants should feel confident on request to offer expert independent advice to government. On legal aspects of governance, this was the job of Solicitor-General Justin Gleeson. Any politician from the PM down had the right to consult Gleeson on legal issues pertaining to upcoming legislation.

However, A-G George Brandis hadn't liked Gleeson's previous advice on several issues, including asylum seeker policy, anti-terror legislation and the debate on same-sex marriage, and most importantly Gleeson had advised the Australian Tax Office to sue for $300 million tax due from Alan Bond's Bell group. The ATO sued and won. But Brandis had evidently promised that $300 million to the Western Australian government, a promise he couldn't now keep. He needed to muzzle the troublesome solicitor-general.

Accordingly, Brandis ruled that he himself had to personally approve any request for independent advice from the solicitor- general. The solicitor-general no longer had an independent advisory role but a political one. Given Turnbull's previous statements about the independence of the public service, he should have overruled Brandis. Instead, there was a Senate committee in which the Coalition attack dogs were let loose on the outraged Gleeson. He resigned, as his role was now politicised and he himself had been deeply insulted. Lawyers' Alliance Australia, representing 200,000 lawyers across Australia, called upon Brandis to resign for this gross breach of principle but of course he didn't, nor was he required to as he should have been.

In late 2017, Brandis was appointed Australia's high commissioner to the UK. His replacement was Christian Porter, whose finer feelings about justice were displayed in his role as Social Services Minister in the Centrelink outrage.

The Centrelink outrage

In a desperate attempt to get at least some money bills through Parliament after the 2014 budget debacle, PM Abbott had proposed the Omnibus budget Bill, a ragbag of financial issues that Abbott claimed must all get through both houses, otherwise Australia would be in deep financial trouble. After some minor amendments, it passed the Lower House with Labor's ill-judged support on the 14 September 2016 – the same day that Turnbull toppled Abbott – and passed in the Senate a day later. It was calculated to save $6.3 billion.

This messy bill allowed Centrelink to claw back what were reckoned to be overpayments to its clients. If the overpayments were genuine, then fair enough, one might think. But they weren't. They were calculated by merging Australian Tax Office data on income with the Centrelink databank. The names on each databank sometimes did not match; worse, the ATO figures were produced by averaging a person's income over a year so that if that person was unemployed for six months and earning for the other six, the average would show that person as having an 'income' while receiving Centrelink payments, which is illegal. But for those six months of unemployment, that person was legally receiving Centrelink payments. Many hundreds of thousands of letters, on letterhead bearing the Australian Federal Police logo, were sent out demanding those 'overpayments' be repaid. The impression was given to the recipients that the AFP letterheads indicated that they were regarded as criminals. That did indeed scare the hell out of many, who were poor, unemployed, part-time workers or students.

The Australia Council of Social Services said that more than 200,000 people had been affected by this campaign and around 20% of the notices were incorrect. People had twenty-one days to challenge the assessment. Thousands tried, but emails went unanswered and phones went on ringing day after day until the poor bewildered clients gave up. If they went to a Centrelink office, staff were instructed not to help them personally, but to direct them to a computer terminal for them to sort it out for themselves, even the old and the computer illiterate. Many paid up, even those who were wrongly accused, rather than pursue what was a stressful and hopeless business. The government admitted that 20% of letters were incorrect but that was considered to be a reasonable margin of error; 121,604 people who had their income support suspended were found to have had a reasonable excuse.

The inappropriately named Christian Porter, Social Services Minister, said that the system had worked 'incredibly well', Human Services Minister Alan Tudge adding that as the government had received back $300 million so far, this proved that the system was working. Tudge evidently thought the sole purpose of this unsavoury exercise was to raise revenue and if it did that, whatever the injustice and human pain it caused, it was a success. In a Senate estimates hearing, Greens Rachel Siewert revealed that 2,030 people had died in the two years after receiving such a robo-debt letter, and that files showed 663 of them were marked as vulnerable. But that is not how Centrelink saw it: a spokesperson told Channel Nine, 'At the core of this is protection of taxpayers' money.' Which is clearly much more important to bureaucrats and to Coalition politicians than driving the least advantaged citizens to suicide.

A year later, Andrew Wilkie revealed that things were even worse. He said that some people were being served double or triple debts because the name of their employer was recorded slightly differently. 'They are hit with debts in the tens of thousands of dollars with basically no explanation and sometimes as little as a few weeks to pay up.' The withers of the Department of Human Services were entirely unwrung. As a spokesperson said, 'The online system accurately calculates debts. People are given ample opportunity to explain their circumstances prior to determining whether there is a debt.'[39] Of course, it's the victim's fault.

Years later, Stuart Robert, who Turnbull had sacked for corruption, became Minister for Government Services in the Morrison government and said the Centrelink operation was indeed working well because '80% of debts issued were accurate'. That is to say, a 20% error rate was taken as evidence that the system was working properly. In any other democracy, that rate of error would be taken to mean that the system was not working properly at all and that heads should roll.

At the same time as the Centrelink poor were being bullied and fleeced, Health Minister Sussan Ley was caught notching up $65,000 odd in travel expenses to conduct private business. She apologised and paid it back, which made it all right in her and many politician' eyes. But soon after Ley's escapade, questionable travel and other expenses were dug up for politicians on both sides, the greater number from the Coalition, including seven members of cabinet. The independent panel set up to inquire into Bronwyn Bishop's gouging of the taxpayer had made thirty-six recommendations that Finance Minister Corman said the government supported. None were implemented.

So the picture in 2016 was that on the one hand the government was screwing the poor and most vulnerable in society, including many who had done no wrong but were accused and punished as if they had; and on the other hand, many senior government members themselves were snatching what public funds they could in dodgy travel and other claims. The situation was unchanged in 2019.

Politicians pillaging the public purse while bullying the Centrelink poor will leave a sour taste in the mouths of voters. One earnestly hoped their mouths would guide their pencil hands come the next election. But they didn't. They re-elected these same shysters and bullies.

The end of the 2016 parliamentary year

The final couple of weeks of parliamentary sittings in 2016 were a shambles. The government with a negligible scorecard to date had to pass something to retain any credibility. On the table were the backpackers' tax, and the Australian Building and Construction Commission (ABCC) bill, neither of which Abbott had been able to get through the Senate.

The proposed backpackers' tax of 32.5% was a hangover from Joe Hockey's 2014 budget, representing a half-billion-dollar budget saving. This tax was far higher than taxes set by New Zealand and Canada, thus severely reducing the chances of backpackers, who are essential in the height of the picking season, choosing to come here to pick fruit. Rural industries were incandescent. They could see their fruit rotting on the ground.

Under intense pressure, the government agreed to 19% – and that was final. Except that it wasn't. Senator Lambie and Labor went for the New Zealand figure of 10.5%. No way, said the government. Senator Hanson suggested 15%, which the government finally accepted, but it didn't pass the Senate, which meant that the tax reverted to the original 32.5%. With only a day or so before Parliament closed, fruit growers with harvest approaching became ever more frantic. In the last hour of sitting, the Greens amended the bill in Senate to 15%, which passed and everyone relaxed. However, to get it through Greens Senator Richard di Natale had traded $100 million for Landcare, which assisted farmers, and 65% of backpackers' super was to be paid back to the government instead of the previous 95%. As Bill Shorten chortled, that had cost the government more than if they had accepted the 10.5% that Labor and Lambie had proposed. The backpackers' tax saga showed the government completely out of touch with the reality of the fruit industry, not to say scandalously incompetent.

But the big one for the government, because they had called a double dissolution on the strength of it, was to re-establish the Australian Building and Construction Commission. When the ABCC debate came up in October, the Bill went through the lower house but the cross-benchers in the Senate played hard ball, gaining amendments that radically diluted the ABCC act, to the horror of the construction industry. So that too ended up as a fizzer.

As Ben Eltham put it,

Any way you look at it, this means that the government's signature legislative achievements of the final sitting of Parliament are two relatively minor bills, neither of which affect the majority of ordinary Australians.[40]

Fruit farmers might disagree with the 'relatively minor' bit, but the point was well made. But it didn't matter, for in October 2019, Judge John Logan ruled that the 15% tax on income, normally tax-free for backpackers who were also Australian residents, could not be levied because that would violate agreements with other countries, and that meant discrimination based on nationality. So it's back to the drawing board on that one.

More woes for the Coalition

Far right Senator Cory Bernardi after only a few months after his election as a Liberal, formed his Australian Conservative Party, to the outrage of senior Liberals. Would the Turnbull government move further right to save more haemorrhaging, or without Bernardi would the balance move towards the centre? We found out the answer in June 2019, when the Morrison government was re-elected. It was far enough to the right now, Bernardi said, and he deregistered the Australian Conservative Party.

With Bernardi's defection, the travel rorts, Trump's contemptuous treatment of Turnbull, Abbott's constant sniping, Turnbull's craven submission to the hard right, by mid-February 2017 Turnbull was desperate to salvage some authority. This he tried to do with a spectacular and deeply personal attack on Bill Shorten: 'a simpering sycophant, blowing hard in the House of Representatives, sucking hard in the living rooms of Melbourne…his knees tucked under the billionaires' tables, what a hypocrite…' That grotesque boys' own locker room imagery – 'sucking hard…on his knees' – was debasing Parliamentary dialogue much more than Tony Abbott's ranting. So much for Turnbull's promise to lift the tone of Parliament, to have genuinely meaningful debates, and no more name calling. He had entered the Ruddian feral stage.

While these playground attempts to show his authority might have delighted his parliamentary colleagues – Barnaby Joyce nearly fell off his seat with hysterical laughter – it must surely have been a nail in his coffin with the public. People hate this sort of thing, and it showed. The two-party preferred poll put the Coalition at 46% to Labor's 54%.

And to round off a horrendous week for Turnbull, the financial figures revealed that the previous quarter had shown negative economic growth – only the fourth time since 1991 that that had happened.

But Labor's handling of the GFC eight years previously was to blame for that. That alternative fact was front page news in the *Australian* (9 December 2016).

The 2017 budget

This 2017 budget had to do several incompatible things: bury the spirit of the 2014 budget but without the extreme right in the Coalition getting stroppy; make Turnbull popular again or he'd be a dead duck; and defuse the weapons in Labor's armoury. Turnbull and Morrison did what Tony Blair did with his New Labor: mix the oil of neoliberalism with the water of socialism. We might call this New Neoliberal, but in the event it turned out more like Old Neoliberal.

Labor wounded the Coalition almost mortally in the 2016 election with their education and health policies. Turnbull's first salvo was to launch Gonski 2.0 with David Gonski himself, who happened to be a friend of Turnbull's, standing on the same platform as Turnbull and Morrison. Like Labor's version, in Gonski 2.0 every student receives the same amount of funding with extra top-ups for those who need more help. All but 251 of the nation's 9,400 schools will have their funding grow by at least 2.5%, and Commonwealth funding will grow from $17.5 billion in 2017 to $22.1 billion by 2021.

Labor was outraged, alleging that Turnbull was cutting $22 billion from school funding. What that meant was that had Labor won the last election, they would have paid $22 billion more than the Coalition. But as Labor didn't win, the Coalition intended to spend $22.1 billion by 2021, which is rather more than was being spent at the time. The Coalition even did what Labor under Gillard didn't dare to do: reduce funding to twenty-four very rich schools, many of them Catholic, to help pay for the extra funding for government schools; 353 schools will be worse off than they would otherwise have been, but over 4,000 schools will be better off, especially those in disadvantaged areas.

As for health, Labor's 'Mediscare' campaign in the last election probably nourished the belief that the Liberals intended to scrap Medicare and move to a US style scheme. To defuse that, the Medicare rebate was increased by fifty cents. with solemn commitments by Turnbull that Medicare was safe.

The National Disability Insurance Scheme (NDIS), another powerful weapon of Labor's, was funded by Turnbull by adding .5% to the Medicare levy and withdrawing the 2% deficit levy from high salary earners. This gave top earners an effective tax cut of 1.5% by 2019, whereas taxpayers on less than $180,000 would start paying an extra half a percentage point on all their income. In effect, the NDIS would be paid for by an overall tax increase. Again Turnbull had encroached on Labor's territory.

So far, the budget seemed to remove the smelly albatross of Abbott's 2014 budget. But not quite. Universities were hit with an 'efficiency dividend', which is a sneaky way of referring to a cut, amounting to $500–600 million to the sector. All up, the tertiary sector lost about $3 billion; students faced an increase of fees by 7.5% phased in over four years, but the time for repaying the now larger debt was brought forward from earning $55,000 pa to $42,000. These proposals came into effect in 2018.

Welfare recipients were to be randomly tested for drug use and, if tested positive, their benefit would change from cash to a food card, but this proposal was dropped under severe pressure. After Morrison's 2019 win, however, it is being revived. The ABC and SBS were facing cuts; foreign aid reduced to the lowest of any Western country, Indigenous Affairs also faced cuts. Climate change was addressed negatively by scrapping the National Climate Change Adaptation Research Facility established in 2008.

Negative gearing and capital gains tax were hardly touched, but that is unsurprising when so many Coalition politicians own investment properties. While 64% of all MPs own more than one property, as opposed to the national average of less than 20%, Coalition members own a staggering 315 between them, one National MP owning 33 different properties. Figures for Labor and other members are much lower. Changing negative gearing on investment properties might well release more housing for the general public at lower prices, but it would play hell with the investments of many Coalition politicians. Perhaps this is why in the 2019 election Labor's proposed policy on negative gearing was attacked so ferociously – and successfully – by the Coalition.

The hardest hit of all in this budget were the young. They would suffer most from the effects of climate change, university fees were even more out of reach for those from a low SES background, unemployed youth faced harsher cuts, and most had no hope of buying a first home, or in Hobart of even renting one. Young graduates would once in the workforce quickly earn that $42,000 pa and more (given the average salary is $80,000) and then they would face paying off their HECS debt, and with ordinary living expenses, home ownership for them too would be pie in the sky. The cut in penalty rates hit the lower paid harder, women especially being losers for they are disproportionately represented in these groups.

Shorten in his reply to the budget did a surgical job in pointing out the lack of 'fairness' in the so-called populist Turnbull budget. If that budget was intended to redeem Turnbull's standing in the polls, it failed: the two-party preferred vote remained stuck at around Coalition 46%, Labor 54%.

Inequality or safety from terrorism?

After the budget, Shorten geared up a notch from accusing the government of 'unfairness' to the harsher charge of fostering 'inequality': inequality between rich and poor, inequality in wages growth (middle and lower class wages having flatlined for years while those of CEOs and other highly paid individuals have soared), inequality in home ownership, inequality between Indigenous and non-Indigenous. All this was typically dismissed by Scott Morrison as 'a lie', but the statistics strongly supported Shorten's case. A 2017 Oxfam report shows that Australia's richest 1% owned 23% of the nation's wealth, which is more than that owned by the poorest 70% combined. In 2008, there were fourteen billionaires in Australia, in 2017 there were thirty-three, which is eight more than in 2016.[41]

Turnbull couldn't win that argument, so with a bizarre front-page appearance, flanked by camouflaged special operations troops in gas masks and porting machine guns like something out of *The Predator Returns*, he solemnly attempted to scare the wits out of us. But never fear, he announced his super-duper counter-terrorism Department of Home Affairs, merging the Australian Federal Police, ASIO, the Australian Border Force, and the Australian Criminal Intelligence Commission all under one minister. None of the agencies involved had asked for this. When Abbott had previously mooted such a Home Affairs department, he was advised not to go ahead. The fact that the new uber-minister was to be the authoritarian bully, Peter Dutton, made it even worse. The outgoing Human Rights Commission president, Gillian Triggs, said that the creation of a new super-ministry of home affairs was part of a hastening trend towards centralised and unchallengeable government power, and was a 'very serious incursion into the separation of powers, the power of the judiciary to make independent judgments'.

Shorten was 'very concerned that these proposals aren't being pushed by our security agencies, they're being pushed by Peter Dutton as the price of him continuing to support Malcolm Turnbull in his job. I'd like to be convinced this is about national security, not Malcolm Turnbull's job security.'

Independent Andrew Wilkie, an expert in military intelligence having been a senior officer in the Office of Assessments, went further:

> Surely this is one of the most nonsensical and alarming ideas to come out of Canberra in recent years…it's more about keeping Mr Turnbull's leadership safe amid threats from his party's hard-line Right faction than it is to do with keeping Australia safe.[42]

In January 2018 Turnbull announced a $3.8 billion fund to enable arms manufacturers in Australia to export weaponry, thus placing Australia in the world's top ten supplier of arms. Our role as an international gunrunner does not make Australia appear a good world citizen at all.

A strange discovery

In February 2018, two locked filing cabinets were sold off in a government disposals shop, going cheap. They were forced open by the unknown lucky buyer to find hundreds of files of top-secret cabinet papers over five successive governments, referred to as the Cabinet Files. On inspecting them, he realised their importance and contacted the ABC who, like the buyer, thought it was in the public interest to publish some of them on the ABC website. Anything to do with national security was excluded. After one day at the ABC, the Prime Minister's Office, from which they originally came, claimed them.

In the papers there were suggestions that Rudd had been warned of safety issues with the home insulation scheme, at which Rudd promptly sued the ABC, saying it was 'lies' as the warnings were not about safety. Tony Abbott was mentioned for handing supposedly cabinet-in-confidence papers to the Royal Commission into Rudd's handling of the home insulation project (ironically this information cleared Rudd from the allegations about safety). Scott Morrison was found to have slowed the processing of refugees' security checks, as mentioned earlier (page 60). No doubt there are more stories to come.

The Cabinet Files publication came when federal Parliament was about to debate a highly controversial new espionage law that would *inter alia* make it an offence to handle confidential information. Thus, if a federal police officer or public servant wanted to speak to a journalist about possible corrupt behaviour, the very act of them speaking to a journalist could make them, and the journalist, liable for up to twenty years' jail. This would easily criminalise some forms of investigative journalism as early as the research phase.

The legislation also requires not-for-profit 'political campaigner' groups like GetUp! to obtain a statutory declaration from donors who give more than $250 a year, confirming they are an 'allowable donor'. Donors who give as little as $4.80 a week will be required to have a Justice of the Peace or a police officer witness their paperwork. GetUp! Director Paul Oosting said,

> This bill serves the interests of the Turnbull government, and no one else. It doesn't stop the likes of Gina Rinehart or the Adani Corporation from cutting huge cheques to their favourite politicians, but it forces everyday people to jump through absurd hoops just to have their say in our democracy.

Had the bill been passed before the Cabinet Files emerged, the buyer of the cabinet – even if he hadn't opened the files – and several ABC staff could have got twenty years in gaol.

Still another fiasco: citizenship this time

Section 44 of the Australian Constitution says that any person who breaches a number of provisions shall be incapable of being chosen or of sitting as a senator or as a member of the House of Representatives. The most important provision affecting the Australian government emerged in mid-2017 when Greens Senator Scott Ludlum, closely followed by fellow Green Senator Larissa Waters, decided that the provision 'any acknowledgement of allegiance, obedience, or adherence to a foreign power, or is a subject or a citizen or entitled to the rights or privileges of a subject or a citizen of a foreign power' applied to them: Ludlum had been born in New Zealand and Waters in Canada, making them eligible for New Zealand and Canadian citizenship respectively. No matter that Larissa was a couple of months old at the time and that the provision of citizen by birth had been repealed by Canada months after that, they both decided they had better resign and let the High Court decide their eligibility for parliament.

Turnbull was delighted, chortling at the 'extraordinary negligence' of the Greens. For it is incumbent on all parliamentarians to have renounced any possibility of citizenship of another country and have all the paperwork done and dusted by the time they are nominated for election. Turnbull's was a chortle too soon. Matt Canavan thought he might be Italian; he too was referred to the High Court but he only resigned from the front bench, not from Parliament itself as the two Greens had done. Canavan was later cleared by the High Court.

Enquiries from the Fairfax media led a staffer of Penny Wong to ask a NZ Labour member what the New Zealand rules of citizenship were. No names, no pack drill. Having a New Zealand parent made someone eligible for New Zealand citizen was the reply. And who had a New Zealand parent? None other than deputy PM Barnaby Joyce. The Coalition accused Labor of 'treason', Julie Bishop asserting that as Foreign Minister, 'I would find it very difficult to build trust with members of a political party that had been used by the Australian Labor Party to seek to undermine the Australian Government.' The fault of course was not with the Australian or the New Zealand Labor parties but with Joyce's sloppiness in not checking his eligibility before putting himself forward as a candidate for election. Unlike Canavan, he didn't even step down from his portfolios, still less resign from Parliament. Turnbull announced to Parliament that Barnaby was not a dual citizen, 'And the High Court shall so decide!' he declared authoritatively. But the High Court didn't so decide and Joyce had to renounce his foreign citizenship and go to election, which he won.

Meantime, Nationals minister Fiona Nash came out as a dual British citizen, One Nation's Malcolm Roberts was born in India and had British parents, Liberal John Alexander was found to be British. The Turnbull government for a brief while was in minority.

It was now Shorten's turn for a chortle at the slackness of these other parties. He gave a 'rolled gold' guarantee that Labor's procedures had been watertight. All Labor MPs were clean. Were they? Labor's David Feeney had renounced UK citizenship but 'had lost his papers': he resigned just before he was due to appear before the High Court. Three Labor MPs, Susan Lamb, Justine Keay and Josh Wilson, resigned from federal Parliament over their dual citizenship. In all, five by-elections needed to be held and, to rub salt into the wound, Turnbull delayed for as long as he could to call by-election day, leaving Labor three down. He called for the by-elections on 28 July 2018, which had already been established for Labor's National Conference. Tough luck, Labor.

The whole business had fallen into nasty party politics, with each major party threatening to refer members of the other party to the High Court. The only sensible way out of this terrible mess, which might affect present and future parliamentarians, was a bipartisan move to systematically check all members of both houses. Neither party was willing to do that. Parliament had taken a ridiculously drawn-out case by case approach in a state of party warfare. It was a plague on all sides – except the Greens, who had done the honest thing in the first place.

And there the matter rests for the time being.

The 2018 budget

The 2018 budget was the 2014 horror budget but with a prettified disguise in the form of tax cuts for lower and middle wage earners, spread over seven years. Built in, however, was flattening the tax rate so that, as Treasurer Morrison said, '94% of Australians taxpayers will pay no more than 32.5 cents in the dollar', compared to 63% if the current system was left unchanged. The substantial majority of savings from the tax cuts would of course go to higher income earners.

Thus, someone on $40,000 per annum would be paying the same tax rate as someone on $200,000. In seven years, those on $40,000 per annum will get a tax cut of $455 but someone earning $200,000 would get $7,225. Morrison saw that as 'fair' because rich people pay more tax than poor people. This trashes the time-honoured progressive taxation system in which those with larger incomes pay a relatively larger proportion of tax.

Also built in was 'a speed limit on taxes' requiring that taxes do not grow beyond 23.9% of GDP. One effect of this arbitrary figure is that if tax avoiders and large companies, who Morrison says he is 'after', start paying tax, there must be tax cuts elsewhere so that his speed limit of 23.9% of GDP is not exceeded. This means in turn that health, welfare and education spending is hobbled. How this fiscal strategy supports 'stronger economic growth' remains a mystery.

The core policy of giving big business $60 billions' worth of tax cuts, including about $30 million to the major banks shown so recently to have been fleecing the public blind, still remained. The government was determined to put this bill through, despite severe opposition from Labor, the Greens, cross-benchers and the public, outraged that the proven corrupt banking sector should receive such a bonanza.

The rest of the budget was all about cuts: 1,280 more jobs cut from the Department of Human Services, when short staffing already means that fifty-five million calls from desperate people trying to contact Centrelink go unanswered. For the really poor, there was nothing: Newstart stayed at $40 a day, which hadn't changed in real terms for over twenty years. People can't live on that. The ABC was due for another cut of $87.3 million on top of Abbott's cut of $254 million in 2014. The managing director of the ABC, Michelle Guthrie, said that the ABC had been slashed to the point where the obligations built into its charter couldn't be met – which, because ABC is the only inde-pendent public reporting on the affairs of government, was no doubt precisely what the Coalition intended. Then there was the $2.2 billion cut to the tertiary sector.

And spending? Yes, $500 million plus for a war memorial in France, $49 million for a Captain Cook memorial at Botany Bay, and $30 million to Foxtel for no evident reason at all. Not to mention the $444 million Turnbull gave in January to the Great Barrier Reef Foundation to help save the reef: it had been unasked for and it was like winning the lotto as one foundation staff member said. The foundation is governed by senior members of the fossil fuel industry and climate change deniers. The appropriate recipients would have been the Australian Marine Conservation Society and the CSIRO, both of which are already equipped for this kind of work.

Turnbull's quality of judgement

Although he ended surprisingly upbeat by the end of 2017, for the most part Turnbull's term as prime minister was one of chaos. Not all of it was his fault. Abbott's sniping was part due to personal spite and part because Abbott was encouraged by the far right who were determined to make life as difficult as possible for Turnbull. Had Turnbull asserted his leadership right from the start, Abbott and his allies might well have been put back in their box, and Turnbull would certainly have gained public admiration for such a stand. He might even have been able to pass the policies that we had been led to believe he wanted to pass – assuming he really did want to pass them.

The citizenship mess was not Turnbull's doing but his handling of it once it had started was maladroit and noisy. No doubt being reduced to a majority of one had panicked him into out-Abbotting Abbott in his shrill personal attacks on Shorten, turning what should have been a bipartisan approach to a common problem into vicious point scoring.

Turnbull's lack of political experience and his at times atrocious political judgement, however, must be held responsible for the most of the chaos. Following are some of these instances of poor judgement: his tax policies, first to emulate Labor's but then to mount a whole election campaign on massive tax cuts for the rich and the corporate sector; his contradictory, callous and mendacious approach to asylum seeker policy; his sycophantic dealings with Trump; his destructive approach to combatting climate change; his backing the unwanted Adani mine; his calling a double dissolution election when he needn't have; the Centrelink cruelties towards the disadvantaged; and promoting the deeply unpopular Peter Dutton and his inhumane policies, giving him more power than any other minister.

One embarrassingly public example of Turnbull's poor judgement was in the ABC *Q&A* programme on 11 December 2017 in which he was the sole guest. His reaction to questioners with a different view to his own was condescending and down-putting. Aboriginal lawyer Teela Reid asked him why he didn't even consider the 'Uluru Statement from the Heart', prepared by Aboriginal representatives at the government's request. Turnbull replied that he wouldn't consider a third chamber to Parliament. Reed replied that this was not what Aborigines were asking for at all; they were only requesting an advisory body. Turnbull then said that the Aborigines already had representatives in parliamentarians Ken Wyatt and Linda Burney, and they could speak for Aborigines. Reid pointed out that these people were elected to represent their electorates, not Aboriginals. Such twisting of the facts indicates either gross ignorance of parliamentary procedure or a lawyer using tricks, including lies, to make his case at the expense of his adversary. The fact that his adversary was a black female and he was a highly privileged white male makes it doubly shameful.

When Barnaby Joyce was busily upholding family values during the same sex marriage debate, he was at that time having sex with his staffer Vicki Campion. That became dangerous, so he got a couple of his National Party mates to give her jobs in their offices at extra salary. There was also a question of travel and accommodation costs for the two. Evidently, public funds had been used by Joyce in conducting the affair, but Turnbull did not want to go down that path: instead he ruled that ministers should not have affairs with their staffers. That changed the debate dramatically from misuse of public funds to one of morality, which alerted the press and others to become morals police. The complications that that misjudgement will surely create have yet to be played out.

As a footnote to the Joyce saga, after demanding privacy for his child during the inevitable media coverage, Joyce signed a $150,000 deal with Channel 7 to be interviewed about his relationship with Vikki. His colleagues thought this a poor show because it is infra dig, if not worse, for a sitting MP to be interviewed for money. Barnaby said that that was OK because it was Vikki's idea, not his.

The leadership spill

The extreme right in the Coalition gave Turnbull no quarter. After hard negotiation, Turnbull and Josh Frydenberg put together the National Energy Guarantee (NEG), which attempted to stem rising energy prices, clarify difficulties for energy companies investing in energy infrastructure, guarantee reliability of supply and reduce greenhouse emissions. Actually, it would have done little or nothing on emissions, and would have stopped investment in wind and solar, but it did promise to deliver significant bill savings to consumers. It was based on modelling that was incomplete, or otherwise inadequate. Surprisingly it was agreed to by the Coalition, and even more surprisingly by the Labor Party. But soon after, Abbott, Dutton, Abetz and other ultra-right-wingers suddenly demanded that the NEG be abandoned.

The government was in disarray – and it was all the fault of Malcolm Turnbull, they bayed. Never mind that the gap between him and Shorten as preferred PM was, and always had been, clearly in Turnbull's favour. In order to establish his leadership, Turnbull called a spill on 21 August 2018. He defeated challenger Dutton by forty-eight votes to thirty-five, but as that was too close for comfort, there were mutterings about a second spill. When Morrison was asked if he would stand, he put his arm around Turnbull's shoulder and declared, 'Here is my leader!' At least he didn't Judas-like kiss him.

Turnbull announced that he would resign the leadership if a spill motion were passed. Dutton got the numbers for such a motion, which Turnbull took as a vote of no confidence and did not stand. Dutton, Morrison and Julie Bishop stood. On the first ballot, Dutton received thirty-eight votes, Morrison thirty-six, and Bishop, by far the most popular of the contenders and the most experienced, only eleven. She was mortified. On the second ballot, Morrison received forty-five votes and Dutton forty.

A conspiracy theorist might look at those figures and conclude that Morrison backers had voted for Dutton in the first ballot against

Turnbull, thus undermining Turnbull, but voted for Morrison in the second ballot. Our conspiracy theorist might then recall Morrison's preselection for the seat of Cook in 2007. He lost the ballot eighty-two votes to eight to a Michael Towke. Allegations then emerged that Towke had engaged in branch stacking and that he had embellished his resume. The state executive of the Liberal Party disendorsed Towke and held a new preselection ballot, which Morrison won. The allegations against Towke were subsequently proved to be false.

Morrison was widely seen as a compromise candidate, agreeable to both moderates and conservatives. Morrison was sworn in as prime minister on 24 August. As it turned out, he was just as hard right as Abbott or Dutton, but with his own take on things.

After thirty-eight failed Newspolls, Morrison – who originally polled below Dutton and Julie Bishop – emerged as the saviour of the government with clean hands, since it appeared that he had not initiated the coup.

How Machiavellian was that? More light might be shown on that question in the next chapter.

5

A Pentecostal Adman for an Unelected Prime Minister

What drives Scott Morrison?

When John Howard became Prime Minister, he'd already had twenty-two years in Parliament. After a few almost fatal slip-ups on his part at first, we had a period of eleven years' stability in government – even if you didn't much like what he did. Then from 2007 we suffered a succession of PMs all of whom had with very little leadership experience, and little experience of foreign affairs. Abbott had a public spat with Indonesia's President Yudhyono over Australia's intelligence service phone tapping both Yudhyono and his wife; Gillard stopped the live cattle trade on the strength of one television programme, to the consternation of our near neighbours.

There are many more examples of prime ministers from Rudd to Morrison driving on their L plates. Most of them only knew or cared about domestic politics. Abbott may have had more experience but he was a loose cannon with his own personal agenda. As George Megalogenis summed up, 'The creative diplomacy that had been hallmark of our engagement with Asia for a generation was replaced by the knee jerk of domestic politics.'[43] It's no surprise that inexperienced politicians will play to voters' domestic concerns for that is what they and their voters know. However, tyro prime ministers should tread circumspectly while learning the ropes, but none of our last line of prime ministers had the humility let alone the wisdom to do that.

Scott Morrison is no exception. His first job was in the Property

Council of Australia from 1989 to 1995. He then moved to tourism, becoming general manager of the Tourism Council of Australia. Next, he became director of New Zealand's newly created Office of Tourism and Sport, Australian Morrison being involved with the '100% Pure New Zealand' campaign. In April 2000 he returned to Australia as state director of the Liberal Party (New South Wales Division). He left in 2004, to become managing director of Tourism Australia. He approved the tasteless but quite successful 'So where the bloody hell are you?' campaign. However, he had personality clashes with Fran Bailey the Minister for Tourism, mainly it seems for not consulting, ignoring protocol and charging ahead with his own ideas. He was dismissed eighteen months before his contract had expired. Indeed, he left both the New Zealand and Australian tourism posts under something of a cloud. That was his background before winning the seat of Cook, also under questionable circumstances as described in the previous chapter.

Eight years later this man was prime minister of Australia.

In the profession of advertising, the aim is to attract attention, to make seductive claims that are likely to have no demonstrable basis in fact – 'Persil washes whiter than white', 'Border security will be weakened under Bill Shorten' – with constant, loud repetition. Advertising requires exaggeration and often outright lying. While Trump thought reality TV was a good basis for politics, Morrison evidently thought that advertising is. Like advertisers, politicians are also trying to change people's minds but as argued in Chapter 1 it should be by using evidence and logic in forming policies not by shouting loud, repetitive and frequently untrue slogans.

But there is more to Morrison's modus operandi than this.

Morrison and Pentecostalism

When first sworn into Parliament in 2008 Morrison declared,

> For me, faith is personal, but the implications are social – as personal and social responsibility are at the heart of the Christian message… [T]hose of us…who seek to follow the example of

William Wilberforce or Desmond Tutu, to name just two. These leaders stood for the immutable truths and principles of the Christian faith... From my faith I derive the values of loving-kindness, justice and righteousness, to act with compassion and kindness, acknowledging our common humanity and to consider the welfare of others; to fight for a fair go for everyone to fulfil their human potential and to remove whatever unjust obstacles stand in their way.[44]

Loving kindness, justice, righteousness, considering the welfare of others, fighting for a fair go are hardly the qualities he has displayed either in his roles as Immigration Minister, as Treasurer, or as Prime Minister. So how does he reconcile his speech with his behavior?

Julian Burnside said that he cannot.

Morrison's conduct as immigration minister is impossible to reconcile with his stated Christian beliefs. He visited the detention centre at Manus Island on September 26, 2013, and delivered a clear message that the transferees would remain at the centre until they went home or resettled in a country other than Australia. This stands awkwardly alongside a passage from Matthew 25:35: 'For I was hungry and you gave me food, I was thirsty and you gave me drink, I was a stranger and you welcomed me', a message at the heart of the Christian teaching he claims to embrace.[45]

Behrouz Boochani, a refugee on Manus wrote a book on his horrendous experiences that won him the $100,000 Victorian Prize for Literature. He recalls that same visit by Morrison to Manus. He said Morrison was aggressive, pointing his finger at individuals, and depriving them of any hope when he said, 'return to your countries or you will remain on Manus forever'.[46]

The Christian faith that Morrison professes is not that of his heroes William Wilberforce and Desmond Tutu, but Pentecostalism, started by Afro-American pastor William Seymour in Los Angeles in 1906. There are different varieties of Pentecostals but the majority believe that the Bible is literally true, that the devil exists and mostly runs the world, that Adam and Eve proved that God created two genders only, so that transgendered people are an aberration, in some sense less than human, likewise homosexuals. Believers need to be 'born again' in order to be amongst the 'saved'. A fundamental belief is that Christ will return at any time. Those who are saved will go to Heaven, while those who are not saved will be condemned to hell.

Does this mean there may be no hypocrisy in Morrison's terrible treatment of asylum seekers if he sees his actions as the will of God? Asylum seekers are Muslims or other non-Christians, and, unlike Pentecostals, are not among the saved. This bifurcation of the saved and not-saved involves a 'them' and 'us' mentality, which makes Pentecostalism so easily reconcilable with right-wing populism as well as with raw neoliberalism. Corina Elaine, an ex-Pentecostal, was as a child terrified by the eschatology of Pentecostalism.[47] She points out that such beliefs in the imminent end of the world would mean that taking action on climate change is unnecessary, even a challenge to God's will.

Pentecostals also believe in 'prosperity theology': that financial success is the mark of God's blessing. If you do the right thing, God will favour you financially, which makes Pentecostalism a wonderfully self-gratifying rationalisation for a neoliberal. The Harvard Divinity School Religious Literacy Project makes this very clear in saying that 'the religious and spiritual legitimacy of wealth accumulation reinforces a worldview in which financial success is an indicator of moral soundness'.[48] The converse also applies. The poor must be deservedly so because they are out of favour with God. As evangelical David French claims, 'It is simply a fact that our social problems are increasingly connected to the depravity of the poor.'[49] You do not deserve anything if you are not trying your best for God. Or as Morrison put it in the 2019 election campaign, 'If you have a go, you get a go.' And if you can't have a go because of unfortunate circumstances or for whatever other reason, then, according to Morrison, you don't deserve to get a go. Such a view in the leader of a country has chilling consequences for welfare policies.

Thus, redistributing wealth upwards is not merely a matter of neoliberal economic theory, it becomes a matter of religious principle. Maybe this is why Morrison steadfastly refuses to raise the below poverty rate of Newstart at $40 a day when even members of his own Coalition agree it is too low. This is an interpretation of Christianity that is exactly the opposite of what Christ himself preached. It is not only very bad politics, as I have argued throughout this book, but it attempts to give divine justification for rank selfishness. *Timeline* nailed it with a cartoon in which Obama is complaining to Christ: 'Trump's reversing all my policies', to which Christ replies, 'Evangelists are reversing all of Mine.'

However, prosperity theology is invulnerable to attack from non-believers because Pentecostals don't have a codified set of beliefs. James Boyce explains that instead they claim a purely personal relationship with God:

> …a unique perspective on the Christian experience in which God is so intimately present to the saved and sanctified that he can be felt, talked to and heard at any time.[50]

This has the disturbing consequence that

> Pentecostalism is in fact the perfect faith for a conviction politician without convictions… Policy changes and loyalty realignments can be proclaimed with self-righteous certainty because the proclaimer knows that Christ is always present.

On the *7 a.m.* radio programme, 18 July 2019, Tanya Levin, an ex-Pentecostal, confirmed how Morrison's religion might affect his role as a politician. She claims the church informs every aspect of his politics.

> The most important thing to understand is that his faith cannot be separated from his politics. That's the nature of Pentecostalism. You live it, you sleep it, you breathe it. Your entire mission on earth is to fulfil God's will. If you miss what Pentecostalism is about, you miss what the Prime Minister is about. It's not about

community work, but fulfilling God's work, and is very much about exclusivity and elitism.[51]

And on using Pentecostalism for political purposes, John Wren writes,

> During the election campaign, he was filmed gesticulating and singing loudly at his local Shire Live (Hillsong) franchise… most Australians seem to find this public display of devotion quite disconcerting. Many, including myself, are revolted by it. The Pentecostal church's 'prosperity theology' means they focus heavily on wealth creation. Hillsong's revenue last year was over $100 million and no tax was paid on it. They pray (deliberate typo) on the weak-minded tithing, many 10% or more of their incomes.
>
> Morrison told the Hillsong congregation that we need more prayer in Australia. Frankly, if that's Morrison's solution to our rapidly failing economy, homelessness, underemployment, climate change, skyrocketing power prices and stagnating wages then we are actually in even more trouble than we suspect.[52]

Inviting the press into Morrison's church Horizon to photograph their prime minister at his devotions, singing and clapping to the greater glory of his God, is none of the business of the general public, yet Morrison obviously wanted to make it so. Apart from the jarring egocentricity this displayed, it came awfully close to blurring that important distinction between church and state. In Pentecostal belief, God's law is supreme, therefore it supersedes the law of the land. Given that, there can be no separation between church and state. Yet Christ recognised that distinction: 'Render unto Caesar the things that are Caesar's…'

To summarise, there are two explanations for Morrison's stated religious beliefs being out of kilter with his actions. One is Burnside's: that Morrison is simply a hypocrite, using religion where it suits him and ignoring it when it does not. Alternatively, as a Pentecostal he could truly believe that his mission on earth is to enact his own private interpretation of God's will. I am not sure which interpretation – the hypocrite or the Pentecostal – is the better one for the rest of us when the person in question is the prime minister of a hopefully democratic Australia.

Morrison continually refers to the 'quiet' Australians. This recalls Howard's 'battlers' but there is an important difference. Morrison didn't preach policy, he just, well, preached. 'We're on your side, because we share beliefs and values in common. As you go about everything you do each day…I burn for you.' Mark McKenna suggests that this not a politician talking but a minister preaching to his congregation.[53] They are to keep quiet and listen to the word from on high. Congregations don't criticise their minister or the church. As if to make that quite clear, the assault on the freedom of the press, which includes laying criminal charges laid against three reporters for doing their job, tells us clearly what happens to those who criticise the government. Congregations don't openly criticise their pastor, and neither should Australian citizens.

So be quiet, be good, and do as he says.

A by-election and a state election

Things did not go well for the Morrison government from the outset. The first major test was the Wentworth by-election following Turnbull's resignation. Turnbull had held this perpetually Liberal seat with a 17.7% margin. The Liberal candidate was so-called moderate David Sharma, but he was not moderate enough on things like treatment of asylum seekers and climate change for the voters of Wentworth, many of whom were ropable at the way their favourite politician had been wrenched from them.

Sharma had been an ambassador to Israel and had thought, like Trump, that our embassy should be in Jerusalem not Tel Aviv. Morrison, possibly referring to Pentecostal belief that Jerusalem is the City of God, or maybe to an assumption that there was a high proportion of Jewish voters in Wentworth, and without consulting diplomats or other experts, announced the shift of the embassy to be policy. Australia at the time was doing a trade deal with Indonesia, our large Muslim neighbour; they immediately reacted by placing the trade negotiations on hold. In the end, however, the trade deal with Indonesia was eventually signed months later in March 2019. The PM of our other large Muslim neighbour, Malaysia, said that the relocation would only increase terrorism.

Kerryn Phelps, once president of the AMA, was a local GP in Wentworth well known and well liked. Standing as an independent, she strongly favoured immediate action on climate change and on kinder treatment of asylum seekers: she would bring all imprisoned on Manus and Nauru to Australia, especially given that many were in dire need of immediate medical treatment. Enough citizens of Wentworth agreed with her and for the first the time the seat of Wentworth went out of Liberal hands – although it was a close go – to the enormous delight of moderate Liberals, most independents and most Labor and Green voters. Sharma, however, was elected months later in the general election.

The Victorian state election in November, contrary to poll predictions, saw Labor increase its majority while the Liberals lost eleven seats. State and federal Liberals tried to explain this wipeout as based solely on state issues but given the Wentworth result and the chaos in the first few months of Morrison's term, federal issues undoubtedly played a part.

Treatment of women

Given the bullying, particularly of women, that went on during the dethronement of Turnbull and continually thereafter, several women left the Liberal Party. Julie Bishop said, 'It is not acceptable for our party to contribute to a fall in Australia's ratings from 15th in the world in terms of female parliamentary representatives in 1999, to 50th today.' She added that she had witnessed 'appalling behaviour' from her colleagues in Parliament, but she was shy about naming any bullies or incidents.

Ann Sudmalis resigned on the grounds of such bullying. Her seat of Gilmore was held on a 0.7% margin at the 2016 election. Grant Schultz was preselected for the seat but Morrison bumped him off, replacing him with Warren Mundine, who was not even a member of the Liberal Party. Mundine was at the time a Liberal Democrat and before that, national president of the Labor Party. At that, Schultz resigned from the Liberal Party and stood as an independent against Mundine. Schultz failed but so did Mundine: the winner was Labor's Fiona Phillips.

Kelly O'Dwyer, Minister for Women, resigned for the usual 'family reasons', but she had been very critical of the boysy climate in the Coalition. Lucy Gichuhi was placed in an unwinnable position and threatened to name the bullies, but she has not so far. Julia Banks defected to the crossbench. The Morrison government was now in minority.

Emergency Management Minister Linda Reynolds came in from the outer ministry to take over Steve Ciobo's job as Defence Industry Minister. She proudly asserted, 'To every woman in the Liberal Party today…you don't need to be a quota. If you are good enough, you can get in…I have been appointed not because of my gender but because of my experience.'

So let us look at two examples of Linda Reynolds's political talent. She had said that the government's energy policy was 'incredibly clear' but when asked what the policy was on underwriting coal projects, she said she did not know because she did not deal directly with questions about energy. Neither did she deal with questions about 'wage flexibility'. When asked in a Sky News interview if she agreed with wage flexibility, she retorted 'absolutely not', severely criticising Bill Shorten for raising the idea. But when told it was Finance Minister Mathias Cormann not Shorten who had raised the matter of wage flexibility, and that it was a key feature of the economy, Reynolds said Cormann was 'absolutely right'.

Let PM Morrison have the final say on women. At the 2019

International Women's Day event he insisted that 'we want to see women rise [but] we don't want to see women rise only on the basis of others doing worse'. Do well, ladies, but not at the expense of men.

And the election was only weeks away.

The Murray-Darling catastrophe

In 2007, Prime Minister John Howard announced a $10 billion plan to improve water efficiency in the Murray-Darling river system and to address allocation of water for rural Australia. The *Water Act 2007* (Cwlth) was passed with bipartisan support. The Murray-Darling Basin Authority (MDBA) was setup to develop the Basin Plan, with the primary objective of limiting how much water could be used by industries and communities in the Basin.

The release of 3,200 gigalitres outlined in the Murray-Darling Basin Plan was essential in ensuring the survival of the rivers and restoring the health of the basin. But in 2016, then Minister for Agriculture and Water Barnaby Joyce wrote to the South Australian Minister for Water making it clear he had no intention of returning the full 3,200 gigalitres to the rivers. On 24 July 2017, the ABC's *Four Corners* programme warned that a catastrophe was on the way: too much had been seized by farmers upriver, especially for irrigating rice and cotton, which need a lot of water. There was insufficient for irrigators downstream and insufficient to prevent environmental collapse.

The ABC programme showed clips of farmers filling private dams and on-selling the water at a huge profit, the meters having been tampered with to hide the theft of water. Small operators had been swallowed up, leaving the largest, Webster Ltd, chaired by Chris Corrigan of waterfront strike-busting fame, owning more water than anyone else in the country. The Australia Institute reported that Webster was gifted sixty-one gigalitres from the Commonwealth, and also received $40 million as compensation for future presumed losses. Further deals, mediated by Barnaby Joyce, handed $112 million of taxpayers' money to Webster's Tandou station. But fair's fair: Webster donates massively to the Coalition. When Joyce was Minister for Water, the government forked out $80 million in water buybacks to Eastern Australia Agriculture (EAA), the company where current Minister for Energy, Angus Taylor, had been a director and consultant. EAA then transferred the windfall gain to its parent company in the Cayman Islands, Eastern Australian Irrigation (EAI). EAI was also founded by Angus Taylor.

An Australian Institute report concluded that these deals brought about 'the concentration of power and water in the hands of few people, and their ability to influence decisions that affect their own financial interests, to the detriment of everyone else and the environment'.[54]

In December 2018 and again in January 2019. the water was algae-ridden and deoxygenated, and many hundreds of thousands of dead fish floated on the water, creating a huge health problem. The fish deaths covered a forty-kilometre stretch of the Darling River, downstream of Menindee Lakes. The kills told shocked Australians that the federal and NSW state governments had been irresponsibly neglectful, arguably corrupt. PM Morrison and NSW Minister for Water Niall Blair not surprisingly blamed the drought but at least three separate reports – by the Productivity Commission, the South Australian Murray-Darling Basin Royal Commission, and the Academy of Sciences review into the fish kills – made it absolutely clear that while the drought undoubtedly had an effect, the main cause for the sudden collapse was mismanagement, in particular by allowing upstream irrigation to the extent that there was not enough water left to mitigate environmental degradation.

There were governmental shock-horror reactions at this, probably our worst preventable environmental disaster. How on earth could that have happened? They should have known the answer to that, for the blame could fairly be attributed to federal and NSW governments, and to Water Minister Barnaby Joyce in particular. Yet the federal government had the nerve to label Labor's setting up of a committee of scientists to investigate this vital issue as a 'stunt'.

The voters in the Barwon electorate in the NSW state elections let the National Party know what they thought of its handling of the affair: the National candidate got seven votes, the Hunters, Shooters Fishers and Farmers Party overwhelmingly replaced the Nationals. NSW minister Niall Blair resigned.

More misjudgement, more scandals

In October 2018, the PM Morrison saw no problem in using 'Sydney's biggest billboard', as he described the sails of our sacred Opera House, to promote a horserace. A remark that prompted widespread condemnation, including a massive demonstration outside the Opera House.

Morrison went to Queensland, where some Coalition seats were tight, Dutton's especially. He remade a large bus, his face leering from the sides of the bus, to tour the area. However, Morrison flew ahead of the bus, which later caught up with him in various centres. A reporter questioned him on the expense of an empty bus while he travelled by air. 'But I'm on the bus. I just got off it,' he clarified.

On Australia Day 2019, Morrison ruled that local councils would be barred from holding citizenship ceremonies if they held them on any other day than 26 January. Aspiring candidates for citizenship must be dressed appropriately, he roared. No shorts or thongs, no matter that they are standard summer dress for many Australians. No traditional foreign garb either. Australia Day will never be moved from 26 January. He added, 'The Invasion Day problem could be solved by having a separate indigenous day.' So there.

And in order to celebrate the 250th anniversary of Captain James Cook's arrival in Australia – Cook being the name of Morrison's own seat – a replica of the *Endeavour* will circumnavigate Australia at a cost of $6.7 million. Strange that, for Cook did not circumnavigate Australia, he only visited the eastern seaboard.

On 15 March 2019, an Australian terrorist entered two mosques in Christchurch and opened fire with automatic weapons, killing fifty-one and wounding almost as many more. His motive was racial hatred against Muslims. NZ PM Jacinda Ardern's response was compassionate, completely avoiding partisan point-scoring. 'We were chosen [for this act of violence] for the very fact that…we represent diversity, kindness, compassion, a home for those who share our values, refuge for those who need it.'

Australian PM Morrison commented in kind:

> This horrific event took place and was targeted to one particular community – the Islamic community – in a mosque as they went to prayers in New Zealand. But in doing so, it was an attack on all peace-loving peoples, on all innocent peoples. And that's why we can all stand together in support of our Muslim brothers and sisters who were the specific targets of this attack.[55]

He was praised for these words. However, they rang of extraordinary hypocrisy, for he and Peter Dutton particularly have been using anti-Muslim rhetoric for many years to justify their harsh treatment of asylum seekers. Jennifer Wilson, independent social and political writer, commented,

> Yes, his statement on the Christchurch massacre was word perfect. But what we should find staggering is not its 'statesmanlike' perfection but its breathtaking opportunism. Morrison's ability to switch roles whenever the occasion demands should deeply alarm us, not fill us with admiration… He is an unbridled opportunist who will cruelly and savagely exploit whatever divisions he perceives as advantageous to him, regardless of the human consequences.[56]

Other indiscretions involved not Morrison so much as his senior ministers, Dutton and Cormann. Helloworld is a corporate travel agency run by honorary Liberal Party Treasurer Andrew Burnes. Channel 9 reported that Mathias Cormann had not been invoiced by Helloworld for some personal family travel to Singapore, worth $2,780.82. More important, Helloworld had just won a major contract worth $21 million to become virtually the government's sole travel booking agency, thanks to former Treasurer Joe Hockey. Cormann repaid the travel cost but that was only a minor detail compared to the obvious corruption involved between Helloworld, the Liberal Party and US ambassador Joe Hockey.

When the contract for running the detention centres on Nauru and Manus Island expired in 2018, the previous contractor, Broadspectrum, did not tender on the grounds that they didn't want to damage their image any further. Without calling for tenders, the government offered the contract of $423,000 directly to the Paladin Solutions Group, the head office of which was registered to a beach shack on Kangaroo Island and a post office box in Singapore. The $423 thousand covered only security, not health or food. Paladin paid its local staff on Manus a pittance and delivered virtually nothing. That worked out at $1,600 for each asylum seeker. A nice little earner for Paladin at $17 million a month.

After the election, when Paladin's initial contract was due to expire, it was announced – still without tendering – that Paladin's contract would be renewed, again at $423 million. New Guinea's new prime minister James Marape objected, saying New Guinea should have a much larger share than the pittance paid to locals. Following this fuss, Dutton intimated that the contract would be renewed only on a monthly basis until a better solution was found. To date, that solution has yet to be found.

Why is Paladin so favoured? A whiff of corruption here?

Medevac

Kerryn Phelps presented a bill – 'Medevac' it came to be called – for all asylum seekers who need medical or psychiatric assessment or treatment, and cannot obtain it on Manus and Nauru, to be brought to Australia. Two doctors must assess – either in person or remotely – the patient and make the recommendation for transfer. The essence of the bill was that medical specialists should decide who is in need of treatment, not bureaucrats, who had previously made the decision who was and who was not to receive medical attention in Australia.

The bill was introduced for first reading in December 2018 and passed the House of Representatives with minor amendments by Labor, Greens and independents. It went to the Senate for approval but Coalition senators shut down the Senate prematurely to prevent it being passed.

It was reintroduced to the Senate on the first sitting of 2019. Attorney General Christian Porter tried to argue that the bill was giving the Senate power to provide resources, which is illegal. Shorten quickly scotched that by saying the doctors would be unpaid. The bill was eventually passed by two votes. Morrison stated he would ignore the will of Parliament if need be. To circumvent that hastily conceived and illegal inaction, he immediately announced reopening Christmas Island on the advice of security and border protection officials, adding, 'We're taking this action to clean up the mess Bill Shorten and Labor made yesterday, once again.' The letter of the law could then be enacted because Christmas Island is Australian soil. However, that advice from border security officials was on the basis of the first bill, passed in December, not the amended one which Parliament passed the following February. It didn't suit Morrison's story to acknowledge that important difference. The cost of reopening Christmas Island was over $1 billion, which Morrison then had the gall to say was $1 billion less for the massive flood damage in north Queensland – and that too was Bill Shorten's fault.

But the bill had been introduced by independent Kerryn Phelps, supported by the Greens and other independents, not only by Labor. Hardly Shorten's doing, then. Further, the bill was only about medical treatment of people currently on Nauru and Manus being brought to Australia, subject to security checks. It would have no effect on future arrivals: the original laws on stopping the boats still held. That notwithstanding, in saying that border security was now weakened thanks to Bill Shorten, Morrison was telling the world and people smugglers in particular that Australian borders were weaker, so the way was clearer for more boats. Perhaps Morrison had his fingers crossed behind his back: Please come, boats, for that will smash Labor's credibility once again on border security. And roll on the next election. This was the first time in many years that a sitting government had been voted down, a bitter defeat for the government on a key policy. But Morrison made this a victory: here was 'Tampa 2' on a plate. Typically, he switched the debate. Here was Labor again being soft on border protection.

The inhumanity of the government during the debate and after was on terrible show. Home Affairs Minister Peter Dutton claimed, 'I don't want to see Australians who are in waiting lines at public hospitals kicked off those waiting lines because people from Nauru and Manus are now going to access those health services.' But Australia could easily care for seventy sick refugees and asylum seekers, made sick by our illegally imprisoning them. Morrison repeated the line. Dutton also said, 'It's essential that people realise that the hard-won success of the last few years could be undone overnight by a single act of compassion.' And Tony Abbott: 'I have a lot of respect for the medical profession but we all know that doctors always err on the side of compassion.' Mathias Cormann, Abbott and others claimed the bill would open the door to murderers, rapists and paedophiles. This was fear-mongering based on a blatant lie, because those receiving treat-ment in Australia would be under lock and key, not released into the community. And few if any were known as murderers, rapists or paedophiles. Further, the CEO of Christmas Island David Price and President Gordon Thomson, both affirmed that with only six hospital beds on the island and very basic medical facilities, the quality of medical treatment needed was not available on Christmas Island.

Morrison did a photo-op on Christmas Island, posing outside and inside the old detention camp buildings, waving his arms pro-prietorially, boasting that this would make sure there would be no more boats coming. Observers pointed out that this act could just as easily have been done under a palm tree in Sydney, not on Christmas Island at a minimum estimated cost of up to $2,000 a minute. But the expense was unimportant compared to Morrison's claim: 'People smugglers know when they come up against me they've got a brick wall and when they come up against Bill Shorten they've got an open door.'

But come budget time, April 2019, instead of budgeting the $1 billion-odd for Christmas Island detention centre, Morrison changed that to $150 million. President Gordon Thomson was furious: local businesses, which would have been dealing with the assumed increasing numbers, were outraged at being used for political purposes. Thomson said PM Morrison was not looking after the detention centre or the civilian population, but his job come the next election.

Dutton tried to stymie the medevac legislation by insisting that doctors needed to engage with a patient directly not to come to a diagnostic conclusion on the records in medical files. However, the Australian Federal Court decided that personal contact was not necessary, as when doctors in a hospital make decisions on the basis of health records. Dutton exploded, asserting yet again that this would 'open the floodgates'. He is currently appealing to the High Court to stop treatment on the basis of documents.

Such determined inhumanity is shaming Australia.

Climate change

Morrison has repeatedly said Australia will reach Paris targets 'in a canter', even before his government had any credible climate policies. In a survey of more than 1,200 business leaders, Australian company directors put climate change as the number one issue they want the government to address in the long term. Senior Liberals, including federal president Nick Greiner, had flagged the need for new climate change policies ahead of the May election. Morrison, an erstwhile climate change denier, had to do something. Accordingly, in February 2019 he launched a new pre-election climate change policy, pledging $2 billion for projects 'to bring down Australia's emissions'.

The policy, the $2 billion Climate Solutions Fund, is a rebadged version of former PM Tony Abbott's Emissions Reduction Fund, which expert opinion deemed not only wildly extravagant but virtually useless in bringing down emissions. That didn't stop Morrison from claiming that the new scheme would play a 'key role' in helping Australia meet the commitment to reduce emissions by 2030. He elaborated that the ERF had delivered 193 million tonnes of emissions reductions so far and the new scheme would beat the 2030 target by 'hundreds of millions of tonnes… It's been an incredibly successful program, both improving the economy and supporting the environment.'

But meeting the 2030 commitment of a 26% cut by 2030, based on 2005 levels, relies on counting old credits, left over from the Kyoto targets, which themselves are based on a credit for stopping land clearing and reforestation. That has nothing to do with the Paris target.

On the ABC's Insiders programme (3 March 2019) Energy Minister Angus Taylor repeated Morrison's claim that the most recent figures showed that the government's policies were lowering carbon emissions. True, the figures were actually declining in the last quarter of 2018 but, as Barrie Cassidy pointed out, they had been going steadily up since 2013 under the Coalition government. The figures of declining emissions for that 2018 quarter were because more households were installing solar panels. Under Gillard's carbon pricing in 2010, carbon emissions went steadily down until 2014, when Abbott scrapped carbon pricing for his ERS, and emissions have been increasing every year since. There is no way the Morrison's ERS and reforestation scheme will meet the 2030 target: the estimate is that it will be exceeded 'by well over a billion tonnes'.[57]

When asked by reporter Chris Uhlmann, 'Have emissions gone up or down?' Minister for the Environment Melissa Price answered, 'If you look at the data over the last quarter they've gone down.'

'But over the year emissions have gone up,' Uhlmann pointed out.

'Well, I'm focused on the good news,' snapped Price and walked off.

Shadow Climate Change Minister Mark Butler said a Labor government would scrap the prime minister's policy. 'The question really here is whether people would trust a Government that has spent five years trashing climate policy, trashing climate science, led by a Prime Minister who brought a lump of coal into the Parliament, suddenly to have had some last-minute conversion in the shadow of an election campaign to take climate change seriously.'

Criminologist Professor Rob White said that having the fore-knowledge that coal is causing demonstrable harm to the environment and then lying about the relevant facts amounts to a criminal act: he called it 'ecocide', for the very life of the planet is at stake.[58]

In that analysis, most members of the Morrison government were and still are guilty of the crime of ecocide.

The defections

Seven members of Cabinet resigned or announced their intention not to stand in the 2019 elections: Julie Bishop, Steve Ciobo, Michael Keenan, Christopher Pyne, Kelly O'Dwyer, Nigel Scullion and Craig Laundy. Most cited 'family reasons' or 'I've been here long enough, time to get some young blood...' None of them mentioned the fact that if the Coalition lost the next election, which many Liberals then feared, the salary of a cabinet member would reduce to $250K as a shadow minister instead of some $350K. Further, the pension on retiring is 60% of the average salary over the last three years. Factor that in and you have a very good reason for getting out while the going's good, family reasons or no.

As it turned out, however, that wasn't the reason for Christopher Pyne and Julie Bishop: they had much bigger fish to fry. Pyne, when Defence Minister, invested $200 billion in the military sector: days after resigning he walked into a job with Ernst and Young to provide 'strategic advice as the firm looks to expand in the defence industry'. Ernst and Young had already received around $100 million a year in government contracts. As Foreign Minister, Julie Bishop privatised foreign aid spending contracts to companies like Palladium, one of the biggest beneficiaries, with contracts around $500 million. Pyne and Bishop were in flagrant breach of ministerial standards. When leaving a ministry, the rule is that you can't be employed by an industry where information gained while a minister can be made available in the commercial sector until eighteen months after leaving government. Canada more sensibly makes that five years after leaving, just to make sure knowledge gained while in government isn't sold to the private sector.

For Bishop, there was also a push factor. In the leadership spill (see previous chapter), she was assured of twenty-eight votes and expected to win the leadership. She was the longest-serving member in the Coalition, was deputy PM, was seen to have had a successful run as foreign minister and, most of all, among voters she was the most popular possibility as prime minister. However, her erstwhile friend, Christopher Pyne, thought Morrison would have a better chance against Dutton than she would have had, so her friend Pyne persuaded many of her supporters to back Morrison, leaving her with an insulting eleven votes and leaving us with the unpleasant Mr Morrison to lead the country. Bishop later claimed that had she been elected leader she would have easily beaten Shorten in the upcoming election. Many in the ALP thought so too.

While these seven defections must surely have worried Morrison with an election looming, all of the defectors were moderates, leaving the government much further to the right. This leaves a possibility that moderate liberals – the Menzians, one might say – could well merge with several independents like Phelps and Banks to form a new middle-of-the-road and likely very popular Liberal Party, leaving an unelectable rump of extreme rightists in the ruins of the so-called 'Liberal' Party.

Another outcome, which very few then thought possible, was that the unelectable rump of extreme rightists was in fact electable.

The 2019 budget

Days before announcing the 2019 election, Morrison and Treasurer Frydenberg brought down the 2019 budget. It was clearly meant to be an election sweetener, with 'the biggest tax cuts in 25 years' brought down in three stages; by the time the final stage is implemented, there will be an essentially flat tax of 30% for those earning between $45,000 and $200,000. This is a significant reversal of the hitherto important principle of a progressive tax system, meaning the more you earn the proportionately more tax you pay. The first stage and second stages give tax relief for low to middle income earners, which all parties agree to. However, the third stage, effective mid-2024, would deliver cuts of $11,000 per annum for the richest and would cost $18 billion in 2024 alone, the overall cost over ten years reckoned to be $158 billion, a massive loss to the Treasury.

Despite this heavy tax loss, Frydenberg still promised to deliver a surplus and not cut government spending. Many economists warned this was simply not possible and that spending in the public sector would have to be cut severely. The University of Canberra's National Centre for Social and Economic Modelling found that 'individuals with high incomes will benefit the most' from the personal tax cuts, while 'a segment of the most vulnerable population, the unemployed people and the pensioners, will not benefit or benefit very little'. Yet Frydenberg and Cormann still insisted that because of their prudent spending and sound economic management, they would be able to return the budget to surplus in the current financial year.

In his budget reply, Shorten promised $2.3 billion for cancer patients, which would all but eliminate individual patient cost for treatment, guaranteed universal access to preschool education, promised to shore up TAFE and university education and committed up to $10 billion to the Clean Energy Finance Corporation (CEFC), and much more.

And while Shorten was delivering his reply budget speech, Morrison looked extremely bored and kept checking his watch.

Electioneering starts

As soon as the budget was delivered, it was expected that Morrison would announce the date of the 2019 election campaign. Instead, he ramped up taxpayer-funded advertising campaigns for an extra week – for once an election is announced, all parties have to pay for their own campaign advertisements and the Liberals were low on cash. He had saved the party a motzer. A week later, with the strain on party funds eased, he announced that the election would be on 18 May.

Who are the better managers of the economy?

Morrison revived the old shibboleth that Liberals were good economic managers while Labor were feckless and spendthrift. He does not mention that Labor under Rudd and Swan, unlike almost all Western countries, avoided the GFC meltdown in 2008. Or that in 2013 the Coalition took over an economy ranked first in the world; now it is ranked twenty-first. They hadn't produced a surplus in all their years in power and had doubled the debt. The fact that they could claim a near surplus in 2019 was due to rising iron prices, and $4.2 billion left unspent from the dedicated National Disability Insurance Scheme. National accounts figures showed that the Australian economy grew by just 0.2% in the last quarter of 2018, putting annual growth for the year at just 2.3%. Worse, gross domestic product per person (a better measure of living standards) actually slipped in the December quarter by 0.2%, on the back of a fall of 0.1% in the September quarter – the worst such figures since 2006 under Howard. Australia was actually in 'per-capita recession', meaning that the economy would be shrinking if not for population growth, while wages fail to keep up with the cost of living. Living standards were declining for the first time since 1991–1992.

In short, the Coalition's assessment of their management of the economy and of Labor's were straight out lies. Treasurer Josh Frydenberg asserted, 'National Accounts show that the Australian economy grew by 2.7 per cent in calendar year 2018.' But the Australian Bureau of Statistics showed that annual growth at the time was 2.3% in both trend and seasonally adjusted numbers, whereas trend growth over ten years before the Coalition took over averaged 3.04%. Australia's economic growth was slowing down, which is not what Morrison and Frydenberg were saying to electors.

Morrison told The Australian Financial Review Business Summit that 'the bottom 10% of households by income has achieved the highest income growth of any group since the global financial crisis'. In fact, wages have at most flatlined in real terms since well before 2008, whereas high salaries have soared.[59] Finance Minister Cormann agreed with the data, not with Mr Morrison, when he confirmed on Sky News that low wage growth is a 'deliberate design feature of our economic architecture'.

Rather than good economic management, the Morrison government had handed out massive sums without tender: a billion dollars plus a year to keep legitimate asylum seekers in horrible conditions in Manus and Nauru, the totally unnecessary $1 billion on reopening Christmas Island, $423 thousand for little known Paladin to provide 'services' excluding food and medical treatment, $440 million to the Great Barrier Reef Foundation who to date had spent only $800 thousand, and none of that on the main causes of the GBR's problems, climate change.

Labor's case

By contrast, Shorten argued at the same business summit that after five years of wage stagnation, 'getting wages moving is not anymore a war-cry for class warriors but is regarded as the number-one social and economic issue in the nation'. Labor, if elected, would restore penalty rates; make equality for working women a priority, particularly in low-paid feminised industries like child care; and crack down on sham contracting, the rorting of skills visas and labour hire. 'A fair go for all' is how Shorten encapsulated Labor policy, whereas Morrison riposted, 'I believe in a fair go for those who have a go', which leaves the unemployed and those struggling on the NDIS and Newstart right out of the picture, which according to prosperity theology they should be: they were not having a go. As you can tell by how poor they are (see page 81).

Labor's plans for changing negative gearing and arrangements, and cutting the capital gains tax discount from 50% to 25%, would allow it to claw back more than $30 billion over ten years, most of it from the higher earners in a position to take advantage of negative gearing. These proposals had the Coalition predicting with certainty the devastating effects on 'mums and dads', whereas Labor's plans had qualifications and grandfather clauses that would mitigate the effects on the average wage earner.

In line with fairness for all, Shorten promised to change laws to bolster the minimum wage, which is quite inadequate for even a basic lifestyle, to an adequate living wage. Morrison ingeniously distorted this to mean that 'he is going to force small and family businesses all around the country to sack people in order to give some others a few more dollars. That is Bill Shorten's plan for Australia. To set one Australian against another. He is engaged in this war of envy on Australians.'

Shorten announced that Labor would like to see that 50% of all new cars sold from 2030 would be electric. Despite the fact that the Coalition had a similar policy on electric cars, Transport Minister Angus Taylor having obtained $8 million to put fast charge stations along major highways, Morrison shouted that Labor was 'trying to steal your weekend. What Australians have always expressed a preference for is the vehicles that have a bit of grunt and a bit of power, because they like to enjoy the great recreational opportunities that are out there.' Michaelia Cash enthusiastically joined in: 'We are going to stand by our tradies and we are going to save their utes.' David Sharma, the Liberal Kerryn Phelps had beaten for the seat of Wentworth and who later regained it, muttered darkly that Labor's electric car target had 'Communist' undertones, presumably because East Germans were required to buy Trabants, a terrible car. This was 'a new level of shamelessness,' as the *Sydney Morning Herald* put it. Or just plain bloody silly, as I would put it.

Morrison shrilly summed up Labor policy: 'Lies and taxes, that's all you'll get from Labor.' As for lying, he elaborated: 'If Labor's lips are moving, they're lying.' Shadow minister Anthony Albanese more quietly summed up Coalition policy: 'All the Government's got left is a fear campaign because they don't have a positive agenda for governing this country.'

Expectations for the 2019 election result

In February 2019, Labor led against the Coalition in opinion polls, 51 to 49%, but Morrison as preferred PM led Shorten by 48 to 38%. Both patterns were stable over many months right up to election day.

Shorten's unpopularity partly arose from his involvement in deposing both Rudd and Gillard: his hands were bloody, and although that was years ago, it is likely some people hadn't forgotten. As to his presence, there is something about his quality of voice, a kind of drawling rant, his background as a trade union leader (but why not Morrison's background as an adman?), and a look that some people saw as shifty. Collectively, those factors allowed too many people to see Shorten as untrustworthy. Going for him was the fact that since him becoming leader, the Parliamentary Labor Party had been stable. Even more important, he had a good, experienced team. As he told Laura Tingle, 'One of the challenges for the current government is they're on their fourth and fifth ministers in ministries. My colleagues on my side have basically been doing the same job for the best part of six years. You learn.'

As for policies, Labor had strong policies on its own ground: health, education, a 'living' wage for all and, perhaps less popular, modifying negative gearing and capital gains tax. All these should have appealed to the ordinary person, whereas the Coalition is tight-fisted when it comes to the average Joe, and especially to the less advantaged, and lavish to its mates and donors, spraying tax cuts around so that the richest get the biggest cuts. It seemed no contest.

During the campaign, Morrison himself did all the running, Coalition members were simply told to vilify Labor, which they did enthusiastically, and to stick with the message that 'we know what we are doing and Labor doesn't'. Whenever a Coalition member was asked a question, whatever the topic, they delivered a spray against Labor and against Shorten in particular.

Shorten suggested bipartisanship over national issues, such as the Murray-Darling, but Morrison had none of it. He seemed to agree with Abbott in his book *Battlelines*: government is a bitter fight against the enemy, the opposition. It is not about working towards the good of the whole country. Bipartisanship is a sign of weakness.

Social researcher Rebecca Huntley pointed out that a range of polls and surveys told us that the general populace want firm action on climate change, are uneasy about the treatment of asylum seekers, want much more control over gambling, are prepared to be taxed more if that will improve education, health and social welfare, want euthanasia, want a world-class broadband network, want making affordable housing mandatory in new developments, are for same-sex marriage, closing tax loopholes, increasing tax at high income levels. They see political donations as straight out bribery especially by the gambling and fossil fuel industries and should be tightly capped or eliminated. Each of these topics attract approval from at least 60% of the population and often much more.[60]

Shorten's electioneering speech just before Christmas 2018 presented a social democratic agenda addressing most of these issues. Labor appeared to have coherent, well-based and well-argued policies, which were collectively designed to attack inequality and make Australia a fairer, nicer country and a better world citizen. Like most other observers, Huntley accordingly predicted a Labor win.

By election day, the Coalition on the other hand had two firm politcies – the regressive tax plan, and allowing 5% down payments for first home buyers. Their campaign otherwise was to insist that Labor's policies would lead to all sorts of strife and disaster.

A lay-down misère for Labor, wouldn't you think? But that was not to be.

6

A Pentecostal Adman for the Elected
Prime Minister

The 2019 election result

The Coalition moved from minority to majority government by two
seats. Morrison immediately proclaimed his win 'a miracle', as if it
were an intervention by God for one of his saved. This claim should
give us pause. As James Boyce pointed out in February 2019, months
before the election,

> The polls suggest that Scott Morrison will not survive his perfect
> storm. But if he pulls off a victory so improbable, there is little
> doubt that he will also believe that the miracle came because God
> delivered him victory.[50]

How this belief might affect the way the PM governs must gravely
concern non-Pentecostals.

But was this unlikely win a miracle? Hardly. The number of seats
held by Coalition and Labor had hardly changed since Turnbull's slim
victory in 2016. The Coalition vote remained constant overall. Labor's
vote, however, went down heavily in rural Queensland and Tasmania
and Labor didn't make up in Victoria as expected. As in the Victorian
state election, and in the Brexit referendum and Trump's victory, the
polls were wrong: that is not miraculous, just that the pollsters need to
revise their procedures.

There are, however, grounds for real concern about the election
campaigning. We had Party A that was well organised, offered positive

policies that would benefit a majority of Australians, policies that Huntley's research indicated that a majority of Australians wanted. On the other hand, we had Party B that had a very recent history of chaos and division, had essentially only one policy that reduced tax for the already well off, and led an extremely negative campaign by a shouting, aggressive leader who personally attacked his opponents and lied about their policies. Yet against all reason, the electorate voted in Party B. This is what needs explaining. It was hardly the popularity of what Party B was offering.

Morrison's win was a matter of style over substance. His background in advertising did the trick for many people. He shouted strong simple slogans without any evidence for their validity. He is an extrovert, aggressive, certain of his view, and totally ruthless in getting his way. He is a stereotype of a strong leader.

Shorten is more introverted, cautious in his claims and didn't attack Morrison the way Morrison attacked him. Would such a man have the ticker to lead the country? Over half the country evidently thought not.

Two styles of campaigning

Morrison's campaign style bears strong relations to Donald Trump's. Both are blatant liars, aggressive, obstinate, egocentric, use blame-anyone-but-me rhetoric, refuse to listen to advice, and place domestic politics above international diplomacy. Both have policies on border protection and social welfare that are cruel and racist. More than a touch of psychopathy here (see pages 42–43). Trump signalled his 'delight' that Morrison won the 2019 election, as if it was some sort of validation of his own style and policies. Australia and the US are now the closest of allies, he said: so much so that he invited Morrison to a state dinner at the White House, a rare honour, which possibly didn't quite work out as Morrison might have expected (see pages 137–138).

The sheer mendacity of Morrison's campaign is breathtaking. He lied about the treatment of women, about the Murray-Darling catastrophe, about the medevac legislation and Shorten's alleged role in that and in border security, about climate change emissions, about the state of the economy, about jobs and growth advancing under the Coalition, about the Coalition lifting infrastructure spending to record levels. The actual data show each of these is quite false.[61] Previously I noted that the Liberals' lie score was far higher than any other party, with Abbott's the greatest of all at thirty lies. Morrison surely brought this Liberal tradition to even greater heights, but I lost count so am unable to give an exact figure to compare with Abbott.

Even more breathtaking was Morrison's own propensity for lying being projected onto Shorten: 'Bill Shorten is a liar. He always lies.'

Shorten on the other hand didn't bother to call out Morrison's lies about Labor policy. He refused to respond firmly and consistently to Morrison's effective scare campaign. One view is that he wasn't going to play dirty like Morrison by going for the jugular. That is admirable of him but it made him appear tame and unwilling to engage in the sort of feisty style that certainly won Morrison votes. It shouldn't have, but Morrison, having nothing much in the way of policy, turned it into a presidential vote-for-the-person style of election: 'vote for Scott Morrison and you get Scott Morrison, vote for Bill shorten and you get Bill Shorten'. After having consistently vilified Shorten, that tautological simplicity should have alienated voters but it didn't. It made the election a personal likeability contest between the two, with Morrison knowing he was consistently polling as preferred prime minister. That being so, why bother about policies?

Erik Jensen accompanied both Shorten and Morrison on the campaign trail.[62] Morrison played the folksy, daggy dad, a family man who loudly proclaimed his love for Australia – 'How good is Australia?' with arms raised in a victory salute – but he avoided policy except to denigrate Labor's and to insult Shorten personally. Shorten sometimes appeared uneasy, talking often at length about complex policies. Morrison put style over substance; Shorten put substance over style – and lost.

In retrospect, some critics said that Labor's policies were overly detailed and ill-matched, making it appear that Labor was on about one thing one minute and something else shortly after: negative gearing, climate change, free cancer treatment, no tax cuts for the rich, franking credits, and so on. What many people didn't see was that they made up a consistent social democratic package (except for their dilly-dallying over Adani). Morrison's constant battering helped reinforce that piecemeal but incorrect interpretation.

Luke Metcalfe calculated the level of education of voters in the area in which the polling booths are situated, and found that polling booths with the fewest people with a graduate degree saw a swing of nearly 7% to the Coalition, whereas those from most highly educated areas swung 0.5% towards Labor (two-party preferred).[63] That observation is backed up by Stephen Long, who compared Donald Trump's unexpected triumph and Scott Morrison's 'miracle' election win:

> ...disenfranchised blue-collar workers and people on low incomes with less formal education swung the race his [Trump's[way. ScoMo's unexpected success showed the same pattern. Electorates that swung hardest to the Liberal and National parties on a two-party preferred basis had a higher share of voters on low incomes, with low educational attainment, and higher levels of unemployment... Labor suffered a backlash in Australian mining districts, hemorrhaging votes to minor parties such as Clive Palmer's United Australia Party and One Nation. In sharp contrast, wealthy electorates with higher incomes swung Labor's way.[64]

Traditionally underprivileged sections of the population are Labor voters, which shows that Labor miscalculated in presenting its policies in so complex a way that basically only the well-educated got the message. Unfortunately, this recalls Winston Churchill's alleged quote: 'The best argument against democracy is a five-minute conversation with the average voter.'

Most damaging for Labor was its confusion about Adani. When in Queensland, Shorten seemed to be in favour of Adani (if not very much) but when below the border, 'well, if it ticks all the boxes, then yes why not?' That pushed Southerners to vote Green and rural Queenslanders, who wanted the jobs that Adani was said to provide – said by Turnbull to be 10,000 but actually nearer 1,600 – to discard him entirely. In hindsight, he should have come out against Adani, pointing out that the jobs after construction were simply not there, that the profits would go overseas, that Adani had already breached several requirements placed on it and so couldn't be trusted, as its record in India showed, that the damage to the Great Barrier Reef would have destroyed more jobs and income than Adani ever would earn. Such a ploy wouldn't have gained any Queensland votes but he didn't get any anyway, but it almost certainly would have staunched the haemorrhaging of Labor votes down south. On Adani, Shorten came out as wishy-washy, unacceptable both to the right and to the left.

The CFMEU was strongly for the mine, but had Shorten followed in Hawke's footsteps he would have negotiated with the unions. Who knows what agreement he might have struck? But Shorten's feet, nimble as they can be on occasion, were too small to fit into Hawke's mighty footsteps.

Another blow for Labor was Bob Brown's unfortunate caravanserai to north Queensland to tell the miners that the Adani mine was immoral in view of climate change and the threat it would make to endangered species. Unemployment is high in rural Queensland and workers had their eye on the jobs they thought the mine would create. They were not impressed by southerners telling them that what they wanted was immoral, an echo here of Hillary Clinton's calling Trump supporters 'a basket of deplorables'. Brown and his followers may have been right in terms of the science, but politically it was counter-productive.

Other misjudgements by Labor, as it turned out, were their financial policies: to stop franking credits for those not paying tax, and to stop negative gearing on investment properties. Both are reasonable but they were explained very badly, even allowing Morrison to call removal of franking credits a 'retirement tax' when it was nothing of the sort. Removing an existing and logically unfair tax concession is not imposing a new tax. Morrison maliciously generalised from a 'retirement tax' to a 'death tax' – and that alienated many elderly voters. As noted, the Coalition had the added motivation to knock negative gearing on the head because they had so many negatively geared properties themselves. Chris Bowen didn't help when he arrogantly said, 'Well, if you don't like it, don't vote for it!' So they didn't. These policies are subtle and not explaining them was an open invitation for the Coalition to badly distort them, which they gleefully did.

A cloud that perpetually hangs over Labor, and especially throughout this and other election campaigns, is the relentlessly negative Murdoch media. Given that one way or another News Ltd has a near monopoly of the various media outlets – a situation brought about by conservative legislation over the years – a large majority of people were being told how bad Labor is and how wonderful the Coalition. This is outrageously undemocratic but conservative governments certainly won't do anything about that imbalance.

All this is very sad. The idea of an election campaign is for candidates and parties to present their policies honestly and in detail so that we the electorate can make an informed decision about the sort of government we want to elect. The way Morrison conducted the campaign, however, suggests that future campaigns will follow his winning tactic: don't reveal your policies and go for the jugular of your opponents, with whatever lies and insults you choose. That's the road to victory for those who think that nothing else matters as long as you win.

In reviewing Scott Morrison's tactics, an image comes to mind of Skull Murphy in the 1960s World Championship Wrestling series. Murphy was a big brute with a massive bald head whose one major weapon was a stunning head butt. Morrison's one major weapon of shouting loudly to suit what the occasion demanded corresponds to The Skull's head butt.

This is what an adman might do, but is it the right style for a leader of a democratic country?

Tax cuts

The only definite policy taken to the election was to lower taxes at a total cost of $158 billion. Labor and the Greens had strongly criticised the tax bill. The cuts were to be in three stages, the last stage due in 2024, the latter amounting to a $95 billion present to the highest income earners. Labor agreed to the first two stages to stimulate the economy but were bitterly opposed to the largest cuts in stage three. The Coalition flatly refused to separate the stages. Labor was wedged beautifully. In the end, Labor voted for the bill in toto when they needn't have done as Morrison had the numbers anyway. Only Adam Bandt and Andrew Wilkie voted against. A black mark against Labor.

The Senate's vote was crucial to pass the tax bill. If Labor didn't vote for the bill, the two Centre Alliance senators (the old Xenophon Party) and Jackie Lambie held the crucial votes. If the government wanted their votes, there would be a price; the Centre Alliance demanded cuts in gas prices, Lambie demanded the federal government waive Tasmania's outstanding $157 million housing loan. They voted for the tax cuts in the belief they'd won victories for their constituents. As Labor shamefully did vote for the cuts, the votes of Lambie and friends were unnecessary. At that point, Josh Frydenberg said he had only agreed 'to have discussions' with the crossbench. However, in a display of negotiating strength, Lambie held the government to its word, and Tasmania's housing bill was indeed waived.

On the same day that Morrison cut penalty rates for many of Australia's lowest paid workers, he accepted an $11,000 pay rise for himself, bringing his annual salary to $550, 000, one of the highest of leaders of western democracies. NZ PM Jacinda Ardern, on an annual salary of $AUD 444,000 on the other hand, refused a $12,000 rise on the grounds that politicians were already well paid and their wages would be frozen for this year.

The richest now get that $85 billion they think is owed to them, but little of that will flow directly to stimulate the economy. Tax cuts for low income earners would stimulate the economy, although increasing Newstart would be even more effective, as recipients have to spend whatever they have, which at present isn't much at $40 a day: any extra would go straight into the economy. However, Morrison ruled that out. 'We have one of the best safety nets, if not the best, of anywhere in the world,' he lied.

So what can we expect from the Morrison government?

Morrison in a gesture to ward off earlier anti-women accusations appointed seven women to his Cabinet, a record. He also appointed Aboriginal Ken Wyatt as Minister of Indigenous Affairs, to the delight of the Indigenous community. This is a first. All previous ministers have been white males, most of whom thought they knew what was better for the Indigenous community than the community itself. Wyatt is pushing hard following the Uluru Statement from the Heart. He said he wanted the voice of Indigenous Australians to be recognised in the Constitution, and that a referendum to that effect be held within the current term of Parliament. Morrison and his far right colleagues quickly scotched that idea, again repeating ex-PM Turnbull's lie that they were asking for a third chamber, when they were not. They wanted a recognised method to advise Parliament on matters affecting Indigenous Australians, not actually to legislate on them. In that same week, the Federal Court ruled that First Australians should not have a voice in deciding on a proposal to dump nuclear waste on their own Indigenous land. And all this happened in NAIDOC week!

Morrison also introduced a Minister of Housing in an attempt to address the acute housing shortage, but that minister is Michael Sukkar from the far right. David Littleproud as Minister for Water Resources 'was heavily implicated in the Watergate scandal before the election. Morrison has put Dracula in charge of the Blood Bank'.[65] Littleproud later disgraced himself over first denying that horrendous bushfires in early spring were due to climate change, then days later asserted that they were. But, he hastened to add, he was not a scientist. Stuart Robert, sacked from the Turnbull government for corruption, is a Pentecostalist and former roommate of Morrison and despite his corrupt record involving trips to China and his whacking great home internet bills paid for by the taxpayer, is now Minister for Government Services and the NDIS. The latter is grossly underspent by over $4 billion, allowing the Treasurer to use that unspent money to declare a near surplus. The Centrelink scandal, now under Robert's brief and still scamming millions off powerless people, has finally led to a class action against the government.

The ministers charged with making decisions that impact climate change include Angus Taylor, David Littleproud, Sussan Ley and Minister for Resources Matt Canavan, all once climate change deniers. All including Morrison now profess to believe in man-made climate change, but they still act as deniers. Each in various contexts has encouraged investment in new coal, ignored the pleas of Pacific Islanders fearful of sea levels that are already rising and refused to take stronger action on climate change by putting a price on emissions, shutting down investment in more renewables, to name a few crimes that contribute to global warning.

What this suggests for the three years of Coalition government is not pretty. Morrison's 'miracle' has given him enormous authority within the party. As he conducted the election campaign as a one-man band, so he will surely, given his authoritarian character, conduct the business of government in like manner, driven by his Pentecostal zeal. His style of managing matters – charge ahead with whatever means, fair or foul, to do whatever he personally wants to do – brought him down in his two jobs in tourism.

Will the same behaviour eventually bring him down in his job in politics?

So what now of Labor?

Labor has not surprisingly been spooked by the election result, Anthony Albanese acting as if shell-shocked. He attributed his tiptoeing around, not challenging the Coalition, to 'conflict fatigue' in the electorate. More like demoralisation, however you interpret that word, in the Labor Party.

In the first week of the new government, the Senate voted approval for the Adani Carmichael mine. All Labor senators voted for the mine. So twice in that first week of the new Parliament, Labor had collapsed into the Coalition's arms: Labor had agreed to give massive tax cuts to those the rich who don't need them and they backed the Carmichael Adani mine. Not one Labor senator had the guts to cross the floor on either issue. Not one.

To change the metaphor, Labor should be finding their feet at the end of their own legs, not those of the Coalition. So where are Labor's policies on taxing the rich to finance health, education and Newstart? Or on combating the greatest moral challenge of our time, climate change? They are still an opposition and should be offering genuine alternatives to the public, not cravenly sucking up to their victors.

Albanese's pitch for more bipartisanship was thrown right back in his face. The Coalition's top priority after the election has been to wedge Labor wherever possible. This is a strange look: a government should be focusing on implementing positive policies not on tripping up a powerless opposition wherever possible. Labor seems to be at risk of becoming more dysfunctional.

Government ministers continually taunted Labor. Far from crediting the opposition for eventually supporting government bills, the government humiliated them for vacillating on the tax bill, Adani, foreign fighters, the $5 billion drought relief fund, to name a few. Even a bipartisan approach to the worst drought in our known history was rejected. Morrison has taken this as his key issue, which has left many Nationals rather unhappy. On the $5 billion drought relief fund, Labor was under pressure from farmers to back the government's bill.

Agriculture Minister David Littleproud revved up the partisan rhetoric, stoking division by calling out 'Whose side are you on?' Sooner rather than later, Labor must surely get capitulation fatigue and rebound as a genuine opposition.

Labor's review of their policies makes depressing reading. Because they lost the election, several seemed to think that they must ditch their social democratic policies and instead support tax cuts, budgeting for a surplus even at the cost of welfare, back Adani, soften their carbon emissions targets from by 45% by 2030 to 30%. Joel Fitzgibbon even urged the party to adopt the Coalition's targets, but so far such a capitulation has been rejected. We seem to be back to the Beazley days of a neoliberal-lite and ineffective opposition. Labor must know that they didn't lose because of their policies, except perhaps franking credits; they lost because Morrison played a dirty, mendacious campaign. It was a matter of election tactics not of policy. Australia badly needs a genuine alternative to neoliberalism. Labor looking to move to the right from centre left, because Morrison won, is a gutless copout that misses the real point of why they were defeated.

It can only be hoped that as they get over their shell-shock, Labor will return to their core principles and provide a genuine opposition to the Coalition's extreme right agenda

Does winning give a government a 'mandate' to do what it likes?

Annabel Crabb said that 'Mr Morrison genuinely can now do whatever the hell he likes.'[66] Which is true. However, it is not true to say that he has a mandate for doing so: 'New governments who attempt to introduce policies that they did not make public during an election campaign are said not to have a legitimate mandate to implement such policies.'[67] Morrison's mandate was only for tax cuts, and a policy on a 5% deposit for new home buyers. Both have now been passed.

So where will the government go now? As Crabb says, Morrison has the power to do whatever the hell he likes. And on past performance, it won't be anywhere nice for the majority of Australians, including many of those who voted Morrison in.

However, it seems that having got his tax cuts, Morrison doesn't quite know where to go. He has lessened Parliament to forty-four sitting days a year, much less work to do, you see, and wastes time bagging Labor instead of setting out a vision for the country. Legislation has been on a topic by topic basis that is politically expedient at the time. Even drought relief, Morrison's pet topic after his US visit, was fumbled largely because it is intrinsically connected with climate change, which is off-limits for action. He later ruled out any discussion of the drought or of massive bushfires in terms of climate change. There is little sign of an overall guiding framework such as even Howard had. Morrison reacts with ill-thought-out legislation. For instance, the International Mining and Resources Conference (IMARC) in November 2019 was met with heavy protests in Melbourne so Morrison enacted a bill that criminalised protests against the mining industry. The fact that existing law covers any criminality escaped his vengeful mind.

We already have religious freedom, in the sense that people of all religions or none are free to worship or not worship as they please. However, that is being rephrased to mean freedom of Christian organisations to discriminate against LBGTI staff by sacking them or not employing them, and even by expelling LBGTI students. Being Commonwealth law, this will override state laws such as those Tasmania has which make discriminations of any kind illegal.

This campaign was given oxygen when crack rugby player Israel Folau posted on social media that homosexuals, fornicators, drunkards, thieves, and others given to a superfluity of naughtiness, would all go to hell. Rugby Australia asked him to remove the posting. He replied that it was his Christian duty to say these things. RA sacked Folau with years yet to go on his contract. This created an enormous uproar from the Christian right saying it was a violation of freedom of religion and therefore the law needed toughening. But Folau was not sacked for being a Christian, but for breaching the code of conduct regarding player behaviour, which all players agree to upon signing their employment contracts. He was given a chance to take it down but he refused. Nevertheless, the issue raised the whole question of the right to speak publicly about one's religion, and the spurious need for toughening the laws in the name of religious freedom. The odd thing is that most religious freedom calls are coming from the right, whereas Julian Burnside argues that right policies are mostly antithetical to Christ's teachings.[68] This gives rise to an intriguing question: if Christ came back to earth today, what political party would He vote for?[69]

An enquiry into changing family law has been set up despite two previous reports, one recent report lying on the table ignored. The new committee is to be chaired by Kevin Andrews, one of the reactionary politicians on family issues, with Pauline Hanson as deputy chair. This is evidently a sop to win over Hanson's vote, who claims men aren't getting a fair go under present law. Her son had breached an AVO, and access to his child was restricted, leading Hanson to claim that women make up domestic violence stories in order to gain sympathy. So how many women, no matter how genuine their case on domestic violence, would front up to this committee only to be put down by Pauline Hanson? This is one more index of the government's determination to buy One Nation's vote, even at the cost of dismissing domestic violence, and to keep to the racist right.

Industrial relations are another to-do for the government. This will consist of picking up where Michaelia Cash left off, essentially a union bashing exercise, which at this stage looks like a return of Howard's doom, Work Choices.

These priorities, Work Choices Mark 2 and a family law enquiry with a biased membership, are difficult to justify at any time, but especially when the economy is tanking, interest rates a record low at .75%, and with loss of $158 billion in revenue looming through the tax cuts. The future looks bleak, yet the government is in flat denial of future financial problems, and is obstinately dead set on delivering a surplus. With interest rates currently so low, surely the logical thing to do would be to borrow and spend on much needed infrastructure, as the governor of the Reserve Bank, Philip Lowe, has suggested.

The shape of things to come was strongly indicated in a *7.30* interview with Leigh Sales on 10 September 2019. Sales put the same point that Lowe suggested: borrowing and spending on infrastructure when interest rates are low is more important than a surplus. 'An absurd proposition,' Morrison snapped back. 'Look, that is not how it works. The governor of the Reserve Bank is not calling on the government to not have a surplus. That is a ridiculous suggestion.'

Asked whether he agreed with Dr Lowe that firms should be giving employees bigger pay rises, Morrison said, 'We want to see wages increase but we want to see them increase off productivity and we want people to earn more from what they do and be able to earn more from what they do by being more valuable in the work they do.' Ah, yes.

Morrison intends to bring back the cashless debit card for Newstart, which quarantines 80% of their $40 a day welfare payment for necessities. Sales asked, 'People on welfare already feel a sense of shame about that – isn't making something like this mandatory instead of opt-in potentially contributing to that sense of shame?' He replied that it was 'a genuine attempt' to help people manage their resources and ensure there was food on the table. And to get them off drugs and into a job; as he has said before, 'getting a job is the best form of welfare'.

Several things about this interview are disturbing. Like Howard, Morrison loudly talked over the interviewer, raising irrelevancies: the same bullying style he used during the election campaign. Then there are his assumptions, first that most of the unemployed are drug addicts, and second that they would be able to get a job if only they got off drugs. The first is insulting and untrue. The second is simply not possible with an unemployment rate of over 5%.

Sales asked, 'Is the proposal really about getting people off drugs and into jobs or is it about kicking them off welfare and saving the money from that?' Not at all. 'This is about helping people deal with a life-inhibiting addiction that helps them get off that and find themselves in employment where they have more and a brighter future. Why would you question the motives?'

Why would we not, given all of the above?

Who are the real threats to national security?

Tamil asylum seekers Nadesalingnam and his wife Priya fled separately from persecution in Sri Lanka. They met in Australia and married. They were issued with temporary visas and lived in a small town called Biloela in Queensland. They were detained for overstaying their visas in a predawn raid and put into detention with their two young children prior to attempts to deport them. The locals in Bileola pleaded to have them released and returned to their home as they were wonderful examples of migrants settling into the community and doing the right thing. These pleas were echoed all over the country, including the Labor and Green parties, even by shock jock Alan Jones, who said the family has settled into the community in exemplary fashion. However, both Scott Morrison and Peter Dutton said that to use Dutton's discretionary power (which he has often used in the past) would in this case send a positive signal to people smugglers and weaken national security. However, a Federal Court judge ruled that the family had established a prima facie case to remain in the country until a final hearing at a date yet to be determined. Until the case is heard, the family has been in detention at Christmas Island for two months guarded by more than a hundred staff so far at a cost of $30 million

Now let us look at another case involving national security. Gladys Liu was born in Hong Kong but university educated in Australia. She has been a significant force inside the Victorian Liberal Party for fifteen years; as a skilled networker, she has raised over $1 million for the party. She failed twice to become a state parliamentarian. Documentary evidence shows that she was a member of the Quandong chapter of the China Overseas Exchange Association between 2003 and 2015. China researcher Clive Hamilton said that the two bodies of which Ms Liu was a council member were explicitly created by the Communist Party of China in order to exert influence in countries like Australia: Chinese President Xi Jinping calls them his 'magic weapons'. When she was going for preselection for the Federal seat of Chisholm, ASIO advised then PM Turnbull not to attend a meet-and-greet function in Box Hill in February 2018, because the people who Ms Liu had invited had suspicious Chinese connections. She was nonetheless preselected by the Liberal Party and narrowly won the seat in the 2019 election. On voting day, she had put up posters in Chinese instructing voters on the 'correct way to vote' namely: 'On the green voting card, put preference 1 next to the Liberal Party. The other boxes can be numbered from smallest to highest.' These instructions were clearly meant to deceive voters into voting Liberal and are currently the grounds for a trial in the Federal Court.

In an extraordinary interview with Andrew Bolt on Sky News, Liu first said she could not recall being a member of the above Chinese committees. When pressed, she said someone could have put her name in the membership list without her knowledge. Finally, when Bolt reminded her of their function, she did recall that, yes, she was a secretary of one of them for three years, but it was not to her knowledge one of Xi Jinping's 'magic weapons'.

The Labor Party raised this interview in Parliament as suggesting Gladys Liu could be a security risk. At which, Scott Morrison exploded that the Labor Party was using not only a racist slur to attack her but was also a very grubby slur on 1.2 million other Australians of Chinese heritage. Gladys Liu, he shouted, was a great Australian. Bolt to his credit accused Morrison of playing the race card: 'this slur against Labor and others was particularly disgusting'. Penny Wong, of Chinese heritage herself, accused Morrison of hiding behind the entire Chinese-Australian community to avoid saying why he had ignored warnings from national security agencies.

Morrison deemed an honest hardworking Tamil family a greater security risk than a politician with proven associations with Xi

Jinping's magic weapons for breaching security. But with only a slim majority he couldn't afford to lose Liu. His defence was to accuse Labor of racism, his usual tactic of changing an uncomfortable issue to a distracting absurdity.

Press freedom

A bad sign early in the life of the Morrison government was that the Australian Federal Police raided the home of Annika Smethurst, a News Ltd journalist, who had written an article a year earlier foreshadowing government plans to covertly monitor Australian citizens. They ransacked her home, even rummaging through her underwear drawer. A day later, the AFP raided the ABC in connection with the 2017 'Afghan Files' based on reports that Australia soldiers had murdered citizens, including women and children, in the war in Afghanistan. Both raids were said to be 'in the interests of national security', which recall Howard's invoking national security to 'justify' the *Tampa* affair, and Morrison as Immigration Minister banning discussion of 'on-water matters' on the same ground of national security.

The common message to journalists was clear: publish anything critical of the government and we'll get you. Peter Dutton immediately said that was nonsense as the AFP and government were completely independent. But isn't Dutton head of Home Affairs, under which the AFP is located? Surely the AFP would not have undertaken such a raid off their own bat soon after the election. A puzzling feature is that the warrant for the raids was signed by a relatively junior magistrate in Queanbeyan.

Undoubtedly, the Morrison government through Dutton was making it clear that journalists, whistle-blowers and critics generally should keep their opinions to themselves if it involves misconduct by government or government agencies, such as the armed forces. Further legislation was enacted – yet again with Labor's support – such that journalists, their sources, and whistle-blowers would be prosecuted and gaoled. Whereupon ABC journalists Dan Oakes and Sam Clark, and News Corp reporter Annika Smethurst, are to be charged. 'Nobody is above the law and the police have a job to do under the law,' Dutton replied to suggestions that charges against the three reporters be dropped.

To maintain secrecy, Coalition politicians have been warned not to talk to the press, and not to be flattered by invitations to go on television or radio programs, because the media is intent on catching out politicians in order to embarrass the government. Accountability is out the window: the less the public know about the government and its activities, the better. Here is a leaf straight from Trump's book. Press freedom may be the 'bedrock principle in a democracy', as Communications Minister Paul Fletcher insisted in a radio interview, but only it seemed as long as pesky journalists were kept in their place.

A backlash against attacks on press freedom has been building for over a decade with Australia's Right to Know campaign.[70] They made a dramatic gesture on 21 October 2019 when a coalition of Australia's leading media organisations and industry groups agreed that all the major newspapers would print a front page as if it had been heavily redacted, as many FOI claims had been, to let the public – and police and politicians – know that the public had a democratic right to know information that affected them.

The heads of the ABC, News Corp Australia and Channel Nine – an odd assortment from the right, the middle and the left – put out a joint statement with their own demands:

• the right to contest any kind of search warrant on journalists or news organisations before the warrant is issued;

- public-sector whistle-blowers to be adequately protected with current laws to be changed;

- a new regime that limits which documents can be stamped 'secret';

- a proper review of freedom of information laws; and

- journalists to be exempted from the national security laws enacted over the past seven years that can put them in gaol for just doing their jobs.

The reaction by police and politicians so far has been defensive to say the least. Politicians agree of course that the public has a right to know but – always this but – 'no one is above the law'. That dodges the point entirely. It's the law that is inappropriate, which is precisely why the Right to Know group has asked that it be changed.

PM Morrison himself has not yet decided on a course of action in reply to these demands but is resisting pressure to make immediate legislative changes to protect press freedom. Meantime, the ABC are taking the AFP to the Federal Court and News Ltd to the High Court.

Yet, despite the outcry about these raids, on 4 September 2019, the AFP struck again. This time it was the home of Australian Signals Directorate officer Cameron Gill, who deals with foreign signals intelligence, supporting military operations and cyber warfare. Gill is married to Australia's ambassador to Iraq Joanne Loundes, who is also a senior career officer at the Department of Foreign Affairs and Trade. Prima facie hardly a man to be endangering national security. We don't know what this is all about because nobody is saying: both Morrison and Dutton disclaim any knowledge of it.

All major newspapers then printed a heavily redacted front page to emphasise how press freedom has been marginalized. Attorney General Christian Porter in an attempt to soften the look over such prosecutions has said that he would only prosecute in extreme cases and that he as AG has discretion over whether journalists are sued or not for writing/publishing material critical of the government. This has been seen as ensuring journalists self-censor their work so that it toes the government line. A future AG might not be so 'lenient' as Porter. However, Morrison contradicted Porter by saying that no Australian should be prosecuted on 'the whim of politicians'. Senator Reynolds added her two bobs' worth: 'two parliamentary enquiries, the front page of the paper, I think, demonstrates that we do have press freedom'. Well, redacted press freedom anyway.

So let us put this issue in the wider context. Since 9/11, Australian governments with immediate bipartisan support have enacted eighty-two substantive anti-terrorism laws, with a further six bills either currently before Parliament or about to be introduced, each such bill undermining citizens' rights bit by bit. This far exceeds the number of anti-terror laws in the UK, Canada and even the United States. Given all this and our record on press freedom, is it any wonder that the *New York Times* (5 June 2019) labelled Australia the world's most secretive democracy?

No other developed democracy holds as tight to its secrets…and the raids (on News Ltd and the ABC) are just the latest example of how far the country's conservative government will go to scare officials and reporters into submission.

The death of shame

One would think that being caught in so many instances of exaggerating, avoiding embarrassing issues by obvious distortion, out-right lying, even in some cases straight out corruption, certain senior members of the Coalition would be shamed into apologising, even resigning. Not one has.

But it's not just in Australia that politicians are shameless. Jill Locke[71] brought the concept of 'the death of shame' into the political narrative, which British columnist Ian Dunt said explains what has happened in British politics since the Brexit mess.[72] In the UK the Supreme Court, the highest court in the land, unanimously found that PM Boris Johnson had misled the Queen. Ian Dunt said this was a very serious misdemeanour and that in times gone by Johnson, the Leader of the House and the Attorney General at least, would have resigned in shame at being caught out. Knowing that one has broken a convention or law in normal times is shameful, but not any more in Britain, USA or Australia. In other words, in this postmodern populist world, convention, principle and even truth itself have given way to what works, what gets the people in, and what's best for you and yours.

This is certainly true of what is happening in Australia. Not so many years ago, PM John Gorton voted himself out of office as he thought it the honourable thing to do. That sense of honour is totally lacking in today's politicians. Trump is simply a marginally psychopathic braggart and bully who intrinsically feels no shame about anything, it seems, but if you believe that God is working through you, then by definition shame cannot enter into your thinking.

The Morrison-Trump love-in

When Morrison visited Trump in September 2019, Trump pulled out all the ceremonial stops. Trump praised Australia as a century-old best friend and ally of the US, naming Morrison 'Mr Titanium'. Whether Trump knew that titanium is a lightweight amongst metals is unclear: probably not, as such subtlety is untypical of Trump.

Nevertheless, it might have seemed that Morrison was cast by Trump not as an equal ally but as a prop for the Trump theatre. Morrison became a grinning and seemingly approving audience for Trump playing with the idea of a nuclear attack on Iran, and stepping up trade sanctions against China. One almost felt sorry for Morrison for being cast in a role designed so that audiences would see him as endorsing Trump, which commendably he did not over Iran. But he did echo Trump's call that China should not be called a 'developing' nation, with all the trade and climate change perks that go with that appellation, but be regarded as a developed nation. Given that China is the world's second-largest economy, such a proposition does not seem unreasonable, but as China is our most important trading partner, it was not very politic of Morrison to at least appear to have been backing China's enemy Trump. Indeed, China reacted angrily against Morrison for that statement, possibly to the detriment of our trade with China. Morrison also agreed to commit $150 million to be part of Donald Trump's nutball $350 billion US space plan to use the moon as a 'launching pad' to Mars in 2024, to the anger of many Australians, not least drought-affected farmers.

Evading the climate change conference in New York, to considerable dismay back in Australia, Morrison instead inspected a cardboard box factory owned by Australian Anthony Pratt, a friend of

Trump. Pratt had a huge floor space that he turned into a noisy meeting of the Trump faithful to hear their president orate. Morrison was roped in to attend the event, standing beside Trump, grinning and seemingly embarrassed at being seen as participating in a purely partisan campaign rally. This is something a leader of a foreign country should not be seen doing.

Another bizarre outcome was that someone in the White House released the news that Morrison had sought for his mentor and Hillsong evangelist-in-chief Brian Houston an invitation to the White House jamboree but the request had been refused by the White House. Whether this was because Houston had not reported crimes of paedophilia in the church or simply that the White House thought Morrison's pastor had no place in these proceedings is not known. It was a bad call by Morrison however you look at it. He, as is his Pentecostal wont, could not see that the White House visit was a strictly secular occasion at which his pastor had no place.

Having chosen not to attend the climate conference in New York Morrison made matters worse by giving a speech to the United Nations in which he boasted that Australia's climate policies 'will meet our Paris commitments', adding defensively that 'This is a credible, fair, responsible and achievable contribution to global climate change action.' He cited no evidence for this position, for there isn't any; what exists shows that carbon emissions have steadily risen under Coalition governments. He went on to say, 'Our Great Barrier Reef remains one of the world's most pristine areas of natural beauty...protected under the world's most comprehensive reef management plan.' He lambasted those who 'ignore our achievements as the facts simply don't fit the narrative they wish to project...' Just what an adman would say when the facts don't fit the narrative he wishes to project.

He implied that behind criticism of Australia's climate status are evil opponents – 'elements' the Chinese would call them – who misrepresent and gull the weak and defenceless. As for Greta Thunberg, he was brutally condescending, saying she should be in school learning from her betters. He attacked adults who 'facelessly exploit their [children's] anxieties for their own agendas.' Instead, adults should 'focus their [children's] minds and direct their energies... [We] must... let our kids be kids while we deliver the practical solutions for them and their future.' It is precisely those solutions that aren't working and that are making children who do know their science anxious about their future. At the end of this speech, he changed the subject to the problem of plastics in the ocean, seemingly to show what a good environmentalist he really is.

On his return to Australia, Morrison gave a speech to the Lowy Institute that had Trump stamped all over it. He said, a 'negative globalism that coercively seeks to impose a mandate from an often-ill-defined borderless global community. And worse still, an unaccountable internationalist bureaucracy...a new variant of globalism [that] seeks to elevate global institutions above the authority of nation states to direct national policies'. This was a clear echo of Trump's simplistic globalism vs patriotism and a direct hit at the UN and its bodies. Like Abbott before him, Morrison tolerates no criticism from global bodies even though Australia is an official member of such organisations.

And to ramp up the pressure on those who march for action on climate change, Peter Dutton told Ray Hadley on 2GB that anyone on Newstart who marched would be taken off Newstart and 'named and shamed all over the country as criminals'. But surely, all citizens, whether or not they are on Newstart, have the same rights, including the right to protest peaceably. However, adding this outrageous remark from the second most powerful politician in the country to the prime minister's defiant rejection of criticism about our human rights bodes ill for our democratic freedoms.

Soon after Morrison's visit to the United States, the Democrats were launching impeachment proceedings against Trump over a telephone call to the Ukrainian prime minister asking him to dig for dirt on Joe Biden's son Hunter that Trump could use against Joe Biden in the forthcoming presidential election, otherwise $400 million of US military aid might not arrive. A few days later it emerged – again through a White House leak – that in 2016 Trump had asked Morrison to help him dig up dirt from Russian sources about Hilary Clinton. Was Morrison's unusual invitation to the White House payback for Trump's old mate?

Surely more will emerge about Australia's possible role in all this.

So what do we conclude about Scott Morrison's prime ministership?

Since 2013, Coalition governments have been riven with hatred and dissension. Abbott's policies were simply to undo everything Labor had put in place, including any credible efforts to combat climate change. Turnbull started out with good intentions, but was thwarted at every turn by a vengeful Abbott and the far right. Now, under Morrison, we have the added dysfunction emanating from the religious right.

This is a sorry depiction of the current state of Australian politics. But hopefully things will change in the 2022 election (if not before). A recent book by Margaret Simons on Penny Wong paints a contrasting picture of how politics might work.[73] Wong fully expected to become foreign minister in a Shorten government after the 2019 election, so she spent a couple of years studying foreign affairs and in particular the strategies of Gareth Evans, the most successful foreign minister we have had. Times have changed since Evans was foreign minister, so Wong has adapted his approach into what she calls 'constructive internationalism', which is a holistic, ecological approach to foreign affairs. She referred to Morrison's warning against negative globalism as 'disturbingly lightweight', adding that he makes decisions against the national interest for 'short-term political gain'.[74] As a binary thinker, she said, he is incapable of thinking globally. In the Pacific region there are other players than China and America – Australia, Indonesia, Malaysia and others, each country looking for its own best interests – and they need to be balanced against each other. Morrison is doing what Trump does: he views foreign relations through the lens of those who voted for him, not through the lens of Australia's interests as whole, let alone the interests of other players. Wong admits that Morrison is 'the best political tactician in Australia right now' – as the election result shows – but he 'hasn't delivered anything of substance, because that's not who he is'.

So who is he as a politician? Many examples related in this and the previous chapter show a man who makes impetuous decisions without consultation and without reflection on consequences, which is a repeat of his performance in the NZ and Australian tourism industries. Morrison doesn't use argument or evidence to support his decisions. His style is based on self-certainty, which emanates no doubt in part from his religion, while his method of propagating these certainties is to declaim them loudly and aggressively, chin jutting, eyes flaring. His aggressive, declamatory speechifying has the rhythm and the certainty of the Pentecostal preacher that he is. He is like the driver of a school bus who chooses to wear blinkers: he only wants to see what is straight in front of him. He is also hugely ambitious and past performance shows he is a lone player, unrestrained by due process. He also has a propensity to lie shamelessly when it suits. Psychologist Lyn Bender was quoted as saying that Abbott and some of his colleagues had strong psychopathic tendencies, and she included Scott Morrison (see page 43). That fits with the picture painted above.

It is sad that we are stuck with this government at least for the present term. It is also sad that roughly half the country did not see what lay below all that aggressive shouting: that here is a tunnel-visioned bully, arguably psychopathic, who rules with simplistic religious dogmas that have little place in a modern democratic system.

Perhaps the greatest tragedy wrought by the 2019 election result is that people with the quality of thinking and judgement of those such as Penny Wong, who are reflective and do see the big picture, were discarded in favour of the present incumbents.

6

Postscript

I concluded Chapter 6 by quoting Penny Wong, who said that Scott Morrison is 'the best political tactician in Australia right now...but he hasn't delivered anything of substance, because that's not who he is.' However, the story cannot end there. Several issues have arisen since then that tell us yet more about who the man Scott Morrison is.

Morrison protects his ministers when they are clearly out of line. When in September Sydney Lord Mayor Clover Moore declared a climate emergency, Energy Minister Angus Taylor wrote her a you-can't-talk letter. He included a facsimile of the SCC website, which stated that the council had spent $15.9 million on travel for its councillors when the real costs on the website were less than $6,000. The document had been forged, but by whom? Not by Taylor, he swore, nor by his office. By who then? That was for the NSW police to find out. Morrison rang the Chief Commissioner Mick Fuller, an old neighbour of his, to ask if an offence had been committed. On the basis of that call, Morrison claimed in Parliament that it was not necessary to stand Taylor down as minister. Yet the NSW police thought the case should be sent to the Australian Federal Police, which operates under Home Affairs Minister Peter Dutton. And surprise, surprise, a month later the AFP reported that there was no evidence to indicate that the minister was involved in falsifying information. Only a 'low level of harm' was involved; and anyway, Taylor had apologised. So forgery isn't a crime worth pursuing if only a low level of harm is involved – even if the victim thinks otherwise – and if the offender apologises. That seems to be saying that the AFP thought Taylor may have committed the forgery after all.

The Medevac Bill, which placed the decision of whether individual asylum seekers needed medical treatment out of the hands of bureaucrats and into medically qualified hands, was narrowly passed a year ago. Morrison was obsessed with repealing it. He and Peter Dutton had raged that the bill 'would open the floodgates' to asylum seekers. It didn't. Nor had it swamped our hospitals, or exposed our children to paedophiles. Rather, Medevac had been working as it should have; people were healed, lives were saved. Any Australian citizen would be totally outraged if an unqualified civil servant was to decide if he or she was to get by-pass surgery or not. But the Coalition, including four medically qualified Liberal MPs, voted it down. How could these doctors justify abandoning seriously ill patients to decisions made by people with no medical qualifications? Isn't that a breach of medical ethics? Maybe they thought it was only a 'low level' breach: better that than wreck their political careers.

The deciding vote was in the hands of a 'weeping' Jacqui Lambie, who voted with the Coalition on the grounds that she had struck a deal with the government, but she refused to say what that deal was. Government ministers denied any deal had been done. At that, she should have blown the whistle on the government. Not only do we the people have a right to know why she voted for such a nasty bill but her silence blasted her own credibility.

An Integrity Bill, intended to weaken unions and workers' rights – very similar to the bill that ended John Howard's political career – failed twice. Attorney-General Porter promised to bring it back in 2020: the Coalition aren't going to give up on that one. The second draft of a Religious Discrimination Bill was unacceptable to all sides. It was well named, as it overrode state anti-discrimination laws, giving religious persons and institutions the right to malign people of other religions or none. A third draft was sent to Porter to fix. Lengthy discussion on these contentious bills pre-empted discussion and action on the rather more important bushfire emergency, which was dramatically rising at the time.

The showdown on the bushfires started back in April 2019, when

Greg Mullins, NSW fire and rescue commissioner until 2016, and over twenty other fire chiefs wrote to Scott Morrison demanding an urgent meeting because 'catastrophic extreme weather events' would 'put lives, properties and livelihoods at greater risk and overwhelm our emergency services'. Mr Mullins did not hear from the prime minister's office for three months. He was eventually offered a meeting with a lesser official, the climate-denying Energy Minister Angus Taylor. Mullins and his colleagues had made the mistake of highlighting climate change as a major factor in the fires: Morrison was determined – at that time – to deny any such link, so he wouldn't talk to them.

So determined too was NSW Premier Gladys Berejiklian, who ordered bureaucrats attending a conference on adaptation to climate change not to discuss the link between climate change and bushfires, at a time when bushfire conditions were declared 'catastrophic' in New South Wales. In like vein, deputy PM Michael McCormack slammed the climate change concerns of 'inner-city raving lunatics at a time when rural Australians are dealing with catastrophic bushfires'.

When Parliament closed in December 2019, and the bushfires were already raging in three states, claiming properties and lives, a state of high emergency was called. But as the prime minister had already promised his kids a holiday, off they went. Usually, a press release says where a PM is holidaying and who is acting PM in the meantime. The PM's office was asked where he was holidaying but the office wasn't saying where, as if it was a matter of high national security. Or perhaps Morrison knew he shouldn't be galivanting off in an emergency and told his office to clam up on any enquiries. Where was he? In Hawaii; someone had spotted the Morrison family checking in at a business class counter for a Hawaiian flight. The country had been left in the inept hands of deputy McCormack. He was comfortable with that, because acting against the bushfires was 'not up to me, it's the states' responsibility'.

Meantime, Anthony Albanese was visiting bushfire victims, saying that as the emergency affected several states the federal government should declare a national emergency and call COAG together for a joint state-federal plan of action, including coordinating current and future resourcing to fight the fires, bringing in professional firefighters and not leaving it entirely to volunteers, buying more water bombers, bringing in the armed services and planning for an undoubtedly hotter and drier future.

Under pressure, Morrison decided to cut his holiday short. His reaction on his return was to agree with McCormack that bushfires are a state and not a federal matter. The fires had nothing to do with climate change, the PM assured us, and he wasn't going to change the government's policies on climate change that he had taken to the last election. On being asked about compensation for the volunteer fire-fighters, who were leaving their farms and businesses to fight the fires, he said they were volunteers and therefore should not be paid: it was their choice and anyway they liked what they were doing.

On 2 January 2020, Morrison visited victims who had been burnt out at Cobargo. Several refused to shake his hand. One furious woman, who had lost everything, also kept her hand lowered, but he seized it, as if refusing to recognise her right not to shake hands with him. Others urged him to 'fuck off', 'go back to Kirribilli'. So he fucked off to Kirribilli. Hurriedly. Afterwards, he patronised these people saying that as they were angry at losing everything, theirs was an emotional response, which he didn't take personally. To my mind, it looked like that lady and many fire victims did mean it personally.

He was no longer preferred prime minister, Albanese was at 43% to 39%, with Labor leading 51–49 on a two-party-preferred basis. In early December, the Coalition had led 52–48. Be it remembered, however, that the Coalition had won the 2019 election with Labor leading by that same figure.

Morrison ordered the implementation of many of the kinds of things that Albanese had been recommending but without acknowledging that fact. He had hijacked what should have been a bipartisan approach, thus politicising the bushfire crisis. He offered compensation to firefighters for costs of up to $300 a day to a maximum of $6,000 per person if they could provide evidence of what firefighting had cost them. He set up a National Bushfire Recovery Agency to be funded with an initial $2 billion for the families, farmers and business owners hit by bushfires. He called out 3,000 servicemen to help with the NSW fires but neglected to tell Shane Fitzsimmons, commissioner of the NSW Rural Fire Service, resulting in a few days of chaos until the logistics were sorted out. The prime minister's office further politicised the fires by releasing a glossy video, 'authorised by S. Morrison, Liberal Party, Canberra.' It portrayed Morrison as a masterful leader directing armed forces to save a grateful nation in desperate times. A 'DONATE' tag was in the advertisement, but such donations would go not to the victims but to the Liberal Party; the video was hastily withdrawn in the furore that ensued. This unbelievably crass advertisement only reinforced perceptions that our prime minister was all about marketing himself and the Liberal Party, not about the national crisis. The video prompted Kevin Rudd amongst others to say that Scott Morrison was unfit to occupy Australia's highest office.

Lightning strikes in Kangaroo Island resulted in apocalyptic fires that burnt half the island, resulting in two deaths, massive property loss, and millions of dead and severely burnt animals in what was once a national park and sanctuary. Visiting the island, Morrison said, 'Thankfully we've had no loss of life.' A voice interrupted to tell him that two lives were lost. His reply: 'Yes. Two. That's quite right. I was thinking about firefighters firstly.' They were firefighters: volunteers.

Morrison said that he had offered NSW help in November two months previously, to which Premier Berejiklian, who had earlier cut firefighting funding but later was in the front line with the firefighters, had protested, 'Not true. Not true.'

On 12 January, the PM was interviewed by David Speers, host of ABC's *Insiders*. It was a gentle affair. Morrison took the opportunity to spin himself out of trouble. Morrison gave lengthy answers to questions that were different from the ones asked. On being asked if he had made mistakes during the bushfire crisis, he admitted yes, now he would have taken his holidays at another time. He then enthused about the states' 'extraordinary' response to the fires and then elaborated on the 'new' extra-constitutional federal response – as if it was his own grand plan from the start. When asked by Speers why he didn't meet with Greg Mullins and the other fire chiefs, Morrison shot back that he had dealt with the current chiefs, without a nod to Mullins and his colleagues. Speers let that pass.

His first move on returning from Hawaii, he told Speers, was to offer consolation to victims. He hinted that he would consider altering climate change policy. But, and a very big but:

> I'm not going to put someone's job at risk, a region's, a town's future at risk, I'm not going to put up electricity prices to do it, I'm not going to put a tax on them to do it. I'm going to achieve it in the way we've met our Kyoto 2020 targets, meet and beat, and we've done that through better technology, through the policies we've put through the emissions reduction fund, and we're going to continue to do that because it is really important.

He did not mention that Australia had a special dispensation at Kyoto and he is using those credits against the Paris target, thus hiding that our emissions today are higher than they have ever been. It's the equivalent of letting his Sharks football team carry over their winning scores in a previous match as credit for their next match.

He claimed that his government 'has always made that connection [between climate change and tendency for bushfires] and that has never been in dispute'. He had strenuously denied this just a month previously. He concluded, 'No one in the Liberal Party denies climate change.'

Speers had to pull him up on that one. Only days earlier, Craig Kelly made international headlines when he openly denied the existence of climate change and any connection with the fires, calling a British meteorologist an 'ignorant Pommie weather girl' when she drew attention to evidence of climate change. George Christensen praised Kelly on social media for this interview, saying the fires were not due to climate change but to arson. In NSW, less than 1% of fires had been started by arsonists.

It is baffling that Morrison would lie so obviously. It is true that climate-deniers like Joyce, Christensen, Canavan and many others in the Coalition aren't Liberals, but Kelly, Abetz, Taylor, and Dutton certainly are. Perhaps he thinks that the majority of his 'quiet Australians' have such short memories they wouldn't see the inconsistencies in what he says.

Morrison then changed the narrative on climate change. We should 'prove our resilience and adaptability by learning to put up with weather conditions that are hostile to human life'. Not to combat climate change or to cut our emissions, but prove our moral worth by learning to live with the consequences of increasing climate change. That way he can continue mining coal and keep his useless emissions reduction policy of paying-the-polluter, so we'll have increasingly to prove our resilience and adaptability as the climate gets ever hotter. His illogicality on climate change surely springs from his Pentecostal beliefs. If the climate is indeed changing, then that would be God's will, to which all, religious and nonreligious, should be subservient. He could even believe that this is Armageddon happening; locusts next, then the second coming of Christ. He is welcome to believe that, as long as he does not make that the basis of policy for all Australians.

At a Press Club lunch on 29 January, just in case there was any doubt that Morrison might be softening on climate change action, he outlined policies nearly identical to those of Abbott's in 2013. But there was a slight change of direction: 'we need to get the gas out from under our feet', thus telling the oil and gas industry to step up the fracking, the methane emissions from which are eighty times worse than carbon dioxide emissions. So yes, fossil fuel industries, keep up the donations for the next election.

In late January 2020, the Australian National Audit Office's auditor-general released a report with the damning news that just prior to the last election $100 million worth of sports grants were awarded by sports minister Bridget McKenzie to marginal seats that needed a nudge if they were to elect a Coalition member. But Sport Australia had calculated merit scores for each applicant and these were to be used for the award of grants. The auditor-general had found that 330 of the 684 awards, or 73%, had not been recommended by Sport Australia. Many clubs had received awards that were very low on merit points while others with high scores were ignored. The key to making the awards was found in McKenzie's office: a list of electoral seats colour-coded by political party. Worse, it later turned out, some clubs were awarded large grants that were submitted six months after the deadline and had not been assessed by Sport Australia. McKenzie also awarded a gun club $36,000 without disclosing she was a member of that same club.

The prime minister supported McKenzie because, he said, all recipients were 'eligible'. In a Senate enquiry into the matter, the Audit Office found 43% of projects were in fact ineligible. Morrison claimed ministers have the right to make decisions independently of any advice because – in a disingenuous twist to the Westminster system – ministers are more accountable through the ballot box than are civil servants.

Further, the National Audit Office found that the colour-coded electoral seats were bandied back and forth between the PM's office and McKenzie's. The PM had been deeply involved in the choice of projects to fund and not to fund. In other words, Sport Australia, and indeed the applicants, who had spent a lot of time and trouble in preparing their applications, had been wasting their time.

Morrison had to undermine the auditor-general's report, otherwise his government was in jeopardy, for this was not just about Bridget McKenzie but about how ministerial powers under the Morrison government had been misused, almost certainly at Morrison's behest. Also, someone had to be the scapegoat. McKenzie had to go on a charge that affected her alone, and here it was: the relatively minor one of conflict of interest. The look in effect is that McKenzie had done what she was told to do, and then forced to resign for doing it.

Tony Harris, once NSW auditor-general, said that as Senator McKenzie had overridden Sport Australia, it was at least a grave misuse of her powers, and that she may have acted unlawfully. He added, 'The Prime Minister's defence is just unfathomable, it suggests he doesn't understand what ethical behaviour is or he doesn't have the power to impose an ethical format on his own Government.'

To clear the air – and especially himself – Morrison referred the case to Philip Gaetjens, formerly chief of staff to Morrison and current secretary to the PM's Department. His task was to judge if McKenzie (i) had acted within her powers as minister, and (ii) without conflict of interest in making the award to her own club. Gaetjens was virtually required to override the auditor-general, which is a gross abuse of process. Which he seemingly did: Gaetjens ruled that McKenzie had acted within her powers as minister. I say 'seemingly' because that is what Morrison said that Gaetjens had ruled: he read bits out of Gaetjen's report then ordered that the report was highly confidential and not to be released. Gaetjens did, however, release a summary of his report to a Senate enquiry, which criticised the awards for lack of transparency but stated that McKenzie was acting within her rights as minister. So here we have a flat contradiction between the independent auditor-general and the chief of Morrison's office. One could be forgiven for thinking that Gaetjens was first and foremost protecting his boss, but we don't have the full story to allow us to come to such a difficult conclusion.

Another side effect of the sports award scandal and Bridget McKenzie's forced resignation was that the positions of both leader and deputy leader of the National Party were up for grabs. At which point, Barnaby Joyce emerged from the woodwork to put his hand up for leader standing against McCormack. Joyce lost but it seems he will now stalk McCormack as doggedly as Abbott stalked Turnbull, or as Rudd stalked Gillard. The Nationals then argued among themselves about climate change: the moderates saying we must take more effective action against global warming, Joyce and others saying 'you do and we cross the floor'. All this on the first day of Parliament, which originally was to have been non-political, dedicated to the fires and honouring the firefighters and those who had lost their lives.

Before the dust had settled on the sports award scandal – if it ever will – a possibly worse scandal was revealed. Before the 2019 election, $150 million was made available for the so-called Female Facilities and Water Safety Stream (FFWSS), mainly for needed toilets and change rooms for women in regional areas; $132 million of that money however was awarded for swimming pools in eleven marginal Coalition held seats, only 10% of which were in country areas. There were no guidelines for these awards, no applications or tenders, no assessments as to whether they were wanted – indeed, one school in Queensland actually refused the money for a pool they didn't want.

The question must be asked about the FFWSS and the sports awards: did these targeted distributions amounting to a quarter of a billion dollars give Morrison his majority of two seats? It is entirely possible that had Sport Australia's merit scores been used as they should have been, Labor could have won the 2019 election. It would be relatively easy to find out. What seats received grants, how many of those same seats fell to the Coalition and by how much, how do the figures stack up against pre-polling? For example, of the eleven seats that received swimming pools, all but one went to the Coalition. Put the two awards together and it would seem likely that Labor might have won the last election and, that being so, the conclusion is that Morrison had bribed his way to power. In other words, the Coalition had deliberately cheated to win the 2019 election. In that case, there would be strong grounds for demanding that the Governor-General call for re-elections in at least those seats that might have been affected by these awards.

Fun times ahead.

The image of Morrison previously had been of a climate change denier, a carefree holiday maker when the country was in crisis, a man with no plan to deal with the bushfires because he held that that was the states' problem. After such disasters, he had to remake his image. His spin and aggression had served him well in the election campaign, but it is uncertain if his quiet Australians will be gulled by him this time. Probably not. His quiet Australians in Turnbull's old seat of Wentworth are taking to the streets, demonstrating outside Dave Sharma's office, demanding real action on climate change.

His refusing to listen to advice, his mendacity and aggression tell us that who he is now has not much changed from who he was in two tourism jobs from which he was sacked. Subterfuge had gained him preselection for Cook, and very likely in ousting Turnbull. And now he is prime minister, these unpleasant traits are if anything even more in evidence.

He is not a big-picture man, a man of vision. He is a marketeer; he is out to sell, which demands prevarication, spin, subterfuge, even outright lies. Accordingly, he turned the election campaign into a personality contest between himself and Bill Shorten, which is a distortion of what an election is about, which is policy. Morrison displays no overall strategy or adherence to principle that gives coherence to what he says and does.

He has slipped up so much during and following the bushfires that he is not even the great tactician that Penny Wong had said that he was. Beyond that, he lacks political, and some would add ethical, substance. His public display of his Christianity, like inviting cameras into his church to film his singing and clapping, is again all about appearances, not about Christian ethics, which are in his rhetoric but not in his actions. His treatment of asylum seekers and of the poor and underprivileged is contrary to anything Jesus Christ preached.

A leader of a Western democracy must surely be a person of substance and vision, who can lead his government to focus on the good of all citizens, who sees the country's interests as more important than the party and self-interests.

But that's not who Scott Morrison is.

7

Where From Here For Australian Government?

Since the Hawke-Keating era, we in Australia seem to have gone from
stable government, with which most ordinary Australians were happy
enough, to increasingly divided and unstable governments. Let us
briefly review successive governments in the twenty first century.

John Howard (1996–2007)

Howard was elected promising that Australians would be 'comfortable
and relaxed'. Some were, others definitely were not. Very early in his
first term, Howard acted swiftly and decisively on gun control after the
Port Arthur massacre. After that, being comfortable and relaxed was not
how many felt. He introduced $8 billion worth of cuts in his first two
budgets, slashing the public service by one third, replacing them with
party-employed minders, and delivering massive cuts to universities. He
pulled the party further to the racist right to pinch One Nation voters,
and set back Aboriginal rights with, among other things, his references
to a 'black armband' view of our racial history. He authorised the use of
force, including attack dogs, in the 1998 waterfront dispute. In the
Tampa incident in 2001, Howard flouted international law, and lied
that asylum seekers threw their children overboard, thus making the
next election not only about national security but dog-whistling about
race. He won that election, although before *Tampa* he was expected to
lose it. He had broken the bipartisan agreement that race would not be
used for political purposes. He introduced a 10% GST after promising
'never, ever' a GST. He committed Australia to help the US in a lengthy
war in Afghanistan in 2001; and again in 2003, without consulting

Parliament, he committed Australia to George W Bush's illegal Iraqi war that was based on lies about Iraq's possessing weapons of mass destruction. He said the 2004 election was about trust, ironically given his Jesuitical distinction between 'core' and 'non-core' promises, yet he won. His fights with the unions led him to go to the 2007 election with Work Choices, which placed workers at a severe disadvantage, but this was a step too far. He not only lost the election but his seat of Bennelong to Maxine McKew (see Chapter 2).

Howard won four elections, surprisingly in view of his unpleasant attacks on workers and Aborigines. He was accused by Labor of waging a class war, which Howard neatly turned against Labor by accusing them of 'the politics of envy'. He was also praised for eleven years of stability and prosperity; the latter was true for the aspiring middle classes (his so-called 'battlers') but low-income people were increasingly worse off in the Howard years. His style and his mendacity allowed him to win four elections, but it is a stretch calling that good stable government. Donald Horne summed up Howard's style as spreading itching powder across the country, setting white against Indigenous, city against rural, soldier against citizen, rich against poor, employer against worker, and of course right against left wing. He did not govern for all Australians.

Kevin Rudd (2007–10)

Kevin Rudd won the 2007 election in a landslide. His first acts were to sign the Kyoto Protocol on climate change and to apologise to Indigenous Australians for the Stolen Generations. Other policies included the National Broadband Network, the Digital Education Revolution, and Building the Education Revolution. He also dismantled Howard's Work Choices, and withdrew Australia's remaining Iraq War combat personnel. The government provided economic stimulus packages in response to the global financial crisis, making Australia one of the few developed countries to avoid the recession following the GFC.

Rudd called tackling climate change the greatest moral challenge of our times, but talks on climate change at the 2008 Copenhagen conference collapsed – 'rat-fucked' by China as Rudd delicately put it – and thereafter, according to Julia Gillard, he went to pieces. She claimed he was not doing his job, postponing action on climate change, flying into tantrums and demoralising his staff and colleagues. Senior members of the party decided he had to go. She and several others including Bill Shorten held a leadership challenge that Gillard won.

Julia Gillard (2010–13)

Despite the dubious way in which she became PM, Gillard achieved a lot. She negotiated a minority government that survived the full term despite relentless attacks from the opposition and the press, which says much about her negotiating skills. Her government passed the Carbon Pollution Reduction Scheme (CPRS), a cap-and-trade emissions trading scheme. While this was in force, Australia's carbon emissions significantly declined, only to rise again when Abbott abolished the CPRS. Gillard also introduced the national disability scheme, the mining tax, the Gonski education reforms and reduced some unfairness in superannuation tax. The performance of her government was also better than the Howard government's on inflation, interest rates, household savings, personal tax rate, company tax rate, international credit ratings, foreign exchange reserves, current account as a percentage of GDP, and balance of trade. It was a successful government by any standards, and for the present narrative not one that displayed unreason the way other governments considered here have.

Gillard's government had an impressive record, but a disgruntled Rudd sniped at her from the sidelines, and with the help of the relentless misogynistic attacks by Abbott and because of low polls, no doubt due to the public perception of governmental chaos in the party circulated by News Ltd, she called for a leadership spill only months before the 2013 election, no doubt thinking she would win. A poll-driven decision saw the hapless Rudd reinstated, immediately followed by the resignation of seven ministers.

Kevin Rudd (2013)

Rudd's second term ran for only three months because the 2013 election fell due. In his first term, he had allowed asylum seekers to be processed in Australia, resulting in a surge of boat arrivals. In his second term, he flipped 180°, saying no asylum seekers would be settled in Australia, negotiating with Papua New Guinea and Nauru for detention centres. Seemingly in panic mode, in rapid fire he proposed creating a special company tax regime and economic zone in the Northern Territory, a High-Speed Rail Authority and the construction of a $114 billion high speed rail project linking Brisbane to Melbourne, and relocating the Garden Island naval base from Sydney to Queensland.

By this time, the public saw the Rudd-Gillard-Rudd shuffles as grade A chaos and in the 2013 election voted in Tony Abbott PM in a landslide.

Tony Abbott (2013–15)

Abbott had been a highly effective opposition leader, but as PM he was a disaster. Before the election he threw out a swath of promises, such as no cuts to education or to ABC and SBS funding, all of which were broken in the 2014 budget. This budget from nowhere also shocked people for its meanness, particularly to the underprivileged. He also undid almost all of Labor's positive legislation, declared war on any efforts to mitigate climate change, stacked committees and inquiries with extreme right-wingers and climate change deniers. In addition to his far-right policies was his eccentricity, such as knighting the Duke of Edinburgh and eating raw onions in public. When tackled by Kerry O'Brien about his lying, he responded to the effect that if something wasn't in writing, then more fool you for believing him. People, even within his own party, were sick of his unreliability and counter-productive aggression. The latter was OK for an opposition leader but not for a prime minister. In a leadership spill, Malcolm Turnbull was elected leader and hence PM, to the immense relief of most people.

Malcolm Turnbull (2015–18)

The biggest problem Turnbull had to deal with was still Tony Abbott; he and Turnbull loathed each other. In 2009 Abbott had beaten Turnbull for leader of the Liberal Party by one vote. Then in 2015, Turnbull beat Abbott. Despite assurances he would not snipe at Turnbull, he certainly did. Worse, Abbott had a coterie of far right and very vocal allies in Eric Abetz, Craig Kelly, George Christensen, Kevin Andrews, Barnaby Joyce, Peter Dutton and others who formed an un-duly powerful faction within the Coalition. Instead of staring them down, Turnbull tried to placate them, thereby hauling the government further and further to the right and increasingly losing his own credi-bility. In a vain attempt to establish his authority, Turnbull called for a leadership spill. Peter Dutton challenged and lost but only by thirteen votes, not enough to give Turnbull the authority he had hoped to establish. In a complicated situation of side-switching by senior ministers, Scott Morrison emerged from behind in circumstances some might see as dodgy (see pages 89–90).

Turnbull may have been an effective merchant banker but he lacked sound political judgement. He was dead meat from the start.

Scott Morrison (2018–)

Scott Morrison projected an aggressive folksy style rather than explicit policies of substance. He unexpectedly won the 2019 election, which he claimed was a 'miracle', hinting as a good Pentecostal that it was ordained by God. He certainly acted as if he believed it. His only policies, finally endorsed by Labor, were massive tax cuts that benefited the rich more than anyone else, and a 5% deposit for new home buyers. This otherwise policy-free victory left him without a frame- work with which to guide legislation, which became politically expedient rather than policy-driven. To make matters worse, he lost seven ministers before his victory, leaving him with a very weak cabinet. He reappointed Dutton to the most powerful Ministry of Home Affairs.

Both he and Morrison are highly authoritarian characters and after AFP raids on reporters, many are concerned about issues to do with press freedom and human rights. Other concerns are lack of real action on climate change and the fact that the economy is tanking despite assurances that we are in boom times when we are not. Morrison also claims his weak climate change policy, adapted from Abbott's Direct Action policy, is reducing emissions when the data are otherwise. His behaviour over the bushfire emergency and the subsequent revelations of priming of pre-election marginal seats reinforce the view that the future of a transparent democracy does not look good under Morrison.

What does all this say about government in the twenty-first century?

Until Howard's election in 1996, Australian governments of either side could fairly be called social democratic. Neoliberal-lite to be sure, but there was complete acceptance of the need for a sound social welfare system, and land settlements with Aborigines as in the Mabo decision. A general feeling of inclusiveness existed, that the government was governing for Australia as a nation. You knew what the government stood for. Twenty years later, all that has changed.

A symptom of that change is an interesting antinomy in Australian politics exposed by Rebecca Huntley (page 116). On the one hand a majority of opinion in the general populace is what seems close to centre left but our governments are progressively drifting more and more to the right, with minor parties popping up from the extreme right. This contradiction was further exemplified in the 2019 election, where a centre left party offering the very things people had said they wanted was beaten by a populist right-wing party with nothing to offer except tax cuts that far and away favoured the rich.

The contradiction can be partly explained by the fact that instead of a policy-driven campaign it became a personality contest between the two leaders: policies seemed to have been overlooked. Thus, the policies of the current ruling politicians are not representative of the people they are supposed to be representing. Further, the ethnic mixes in the general population and in Parliament are very different. Another factor is that the policies that a majority say they want are not spread evenly over the population. As was clear in the 2019 election, rural electorates that depended on mining put the supposed jobs involved ahead of action on climate change, while urban electorates did not. Gross national surveys do not therefore predict what will happen in specific seats.

Huntley thinks the population in general simply wasn't listening. She put this down to a lack of trust in politicians generally. This is perhaps why a record number voted before election campaigning had finished. What is needed is what she calls deliberative democracy, involving more people in political decision-making processes: surveys show that people want this. Local communities should be involved in selection of candidates as happened she says in Indi, a seat which independent Cathy McGowan took from Liberal Sophie Mirabella in 2013 and is now held by another independent, Helen Haines. I'll be returning to this vital issue of people taking over from politicians.

The problem is, however, far larger than the 2019 election. The single most striking aspect of recent political history is the disjunct between election wins, and what polls, focus groups and the sheer balance of numbers tell us about what about half the electorate actually wants. Howard won four elections, Abbott, Turnbull and Morrison won one each: that is, hard right conservatives have won seven elections. Labor have won only two: Rudd and Gillard have won one each (Gillard's a minority government). Here is a gross imbalance: strongly conservative forces are winning elections at a much greater rate than non-conservatives, when strong conservative policies are not what a majority of people want. Another related imbalance is that the extreme conservatives are a minority in the Coalition, less than a third of all Coalition MPs, yet the extreme right are calling all the shots not the moderate majority. All this surely needs explaining.

Gerrymandering favouring conservatives does not seem to be an issue. Marginal seats, and there are several, however, do favour conservative voters. This was clearly true in the 2019 election of votes in rural Queensland, Northern Tasmania and also in western Sydney: Howard's strong stand on asylum seekers, made even stronger by Abbott and Morrison, appealed to white racists and paradoxically to sufficient recent immigrants who are now settled and don't want any more to follow (as in 'I'm all right, Jack…') thus swinging such marginals the conservative way. Thus, more conservative seats are won for proportionately fewer votes. But even this surely doesn't account for the fact that in the past twenty-three years, seven strongly conservative governments and only two Labor governments have been elected.

Part of the answer is that the right wing controls the popular media. (Or is it that the media controls the right wing?) Perhaps partly because of this, weak Labor leaders have allowed themselves to be wedged. Then crass behaviour by Labor put Abbott on the prime-ministerial throne, and policy-free fear-mongering by the right mixed with poor explanation of Labor policies enthroned Morrison.

These reasons are Australia-specific, but this is not just an Australian problem. George Grundy notes that

Hard right strongmen (they're all men) have taken control of some of the world's largest democracies in a wave of authoritarian faux populism. Trump is perhaps the most extreme, but Bolsonaro in Brazil, Morrison in Australia and Johnson in Great Britain are recent additions to a club that already included Duterte in the Philippines, Orban in Hungary and Erdogan in Turkey…[75]

Grundy lists specific reasons for the rise of these autocrats in different countries. In Australia's case he suggests, 'Australia's current government appears to have been handpicked by a billionaire who spent $60 million advertising his political party without trying to win a single seat.' Specific factors like these can't really explain what is happening globally.

So how can this imbalance be redressed? Grundy points out that dramatic political change typically occurs after a catastrophe. He suggests that when a climatic catastrophe occurs, as is likely to happen if it isn't happening already, the pendulum will swing back from right to left, as it did after World War II for instance. That is cold comfort. And it doesn't explain how the strong men got there in the first place.

It is likely that bullies like Trump, Bolsanaro, Johnson and Morrison get elected because they have the ruthless sort of personality to force their way through the holes in the system, with no doubt the help of vast amounts of political donations by for instance Clive Palmer and his kind.

What are some of the holes that allow bullies to force their way through and is it possible to adjust the system to plug them up?

Presidentialism

James Walter points out that in 1909 Alfred Deakin complained that

> The mischief is that democracy in Australia, as in the United States, insists on attaching extraordinary significance to the personality of its political leader.[76]

Whereas the US political system was designed to have a president, Australia's was not. Yet since Howard, the leader's personality has played a larger and larger role in decision making. Walter goes on to say that effective leadership is a collective endeavour: it is 'beyond the wit of individuals fully to comprehend, let alone deal with, the complexities of the current moment'. We surely need 'distributed leadership', a point Hawke was big enough to grasp, whereas Rudd did not; he was addicted to micromanaging and failed badly. Morrison seems to be similarly addicted and according to all the rules of the game he too is failing.

At least until 2018 the prime ministership has been a structural issue: the PM is whoever happens to be the leader of the party voted into government, and is guided by collective cabinet decisions. Howard started to act presidentially at times – even on occasion standing in for the Governor-General – but Morrison took that much further. He ran the 2019 election campaign not on policy but as a personal contest between him and Bill Shorten. Morrison did most of the campaigning on his own, rather than letting his ministers do much of the running, attacking Shorten personally on whatever ground happened to be current, projecting his own penchant for telling lies onto Shorten. The sad thing is that this personality-based attack worked when, in our system of government, it should be a matter of voters choosing between policies. That is what democracy should be about, but we lost that entirely in the 2019 election.

Secrecy

Hawke and Keating were relatively open in their government, directly seeking public consultation. Since then, Coalition governments have been increasingly secretive. This started with treatment of asylum seekers, hiding what was happening to them under a quasi-militaristic cloak of secrecy: information about boats entering or being forced to leave Australian waters were called 'on-water matters' and top secret, frontline staff were called Border Force and donned militaristic uniforms, thus reinforcing the impression that what was happening to asylum seekers was a matter of high national security. Doctors and paramedical staff, who knew first-hand the conditions in offshore detention camps, were forbidden to tell Australians what was happening in these camps on pain of two years' imprisonment. Journalists, their sources and whistle-blowers were intimidated from discussing anything the government didn't want us to know about, one journalist having her private home ransacked by federal police. All this and more has earned Australia the title of being 'the world's most secretive democracy'.

Mendacity

As we have seen, a culture of lying has characterised the Coalition from Howard ('core and non-core promises'), to Abbott ('if it's not in writing, more fool you for believing me'), to Turnbull (his term was an existential lie as his credibility nosedived as the far right bullied him into positions that seemed against his former beliefs), and to Morrison (as elaborated above).

Authoritarianism and leadership

Bob Hawke could have been called authoritarian but he was also collaborative, which made him a strong leader both well liked and effective. Rudd had strong authoritarian tendencies on and off, but he was not a good leader, too temperamental and prone to tantrums. Gillard was a good leader and negotiator, holding together a fragile minority government full term. Howard, Abbott and Morrison were all strong top-down leaders but increasingly non-consultative. Whereas Hawke governed for all Australians, Coalition governments after him have all been divisive, favouring their base comprising the rich and the corporate world, while anyone on the left, Indigenous Australians, asylum seekers, and disadvantaged people like Centrelink clients have borne the brunt of discrimination by a biased, authoritarian government.

In the last twenty years or so then, we have seen a steady deterioration in the quality of governance in Australia as indicated by authoritarianism, secrecy, wedging by using phony national security scares, mendacity and transforming the prime ministerial style to a presidential one in a system not designed for that. In that time, we have moved from a social democracy, that is rule by and for the people, to what is increasingly alt-right populism, rule by divisive mob manipulation, which includes lying on a grand scale. It comes as no surprise that just 31% of Australians trust their politicians.[77]

How might we plug those holes?

If the governmental system is not delivering for all Australians, what might be changed? A major attempt to do something like this, although not in the terms I have described, is contained in a report drawn up by a collaboration between the University of Melbourne, the new Democracy Foundation and the Susan McKinnon Foundation. They produced the report before the May 2019 election, intending that the winner of the election might pursue them. That obviously won't happen now but their list is worth considering. I have added my comments to their original wording (which is in italics).[78] It has been endorsed by politicians as diverse as former Victorian Labor premier John Brumby and former Queensland LNP premier Campbell Newman.

1. *Review of parliamentary terms to provide more certainty and improve government decision-making.* It is not clear if this includes fixed terms federally, as in some states. If so, this would prevent the government of the day choosing to go to the polls when best suits it. In 2019, Morrison named election day when it best suited his party's finances.

2. *Appoint a genuinely independent Speaker of the House and President of the Senate.* A few speakers are indeed unbiased, but when a Bronwyn Bishop is appointed, Parliament descends into a toxic chaos.

3. *Trial changes to seating arrangements in parliament to encourage more civility and constructive dialogue.* Indeed. Scandinavian parliaments adopt a semicircular arrangement that encourages discussion and dialogue rather than confrontation as at present.

4. *Introduce more 'free votes' in the parliament through a new parliamentary convention.* If this means allowing politicians to vote according to their constituents' wishes and also according to their own conscience, then certainly. But a new 'parliamentary' convention seems to exclude restrictions imposed by political parties on crossing the floor: they too should be revisited. Crossing the floor is allowed but not encouraged in the UK and in the USA.

5. *Real reform on political donations and campaign financing.* Donations should be capped possibly at no more than say $1,000, and donations from businesses, the corporate world and foreign countries should be banned altogether.

6. *More stringent transparency requirements for political parties.* Hopefully this would extend to preselection procedures. Preselection should be carried out by the voters in the electorate, not by factional heavies in the parties.

7. *Trial of AEC-issued candidate information packs that give voters more information about local candidates.* Good idea; related to (6).

8. *Undertake a process after each election that gives citizens a chance to communicate how we can improve elections.* Ideal for a citizens' assembly (see below).

9. *Commit political parties especially during election campaigns to the same standards that companies are bound by when they advertise, to promote better truth in advertising.* Not only truth in advertising; politicians should abide by the same rules in Parliament as well as outside it. A strict code of ethics for politicians, banning unseemly parliamentary behaviour and outright lying, is badly needed. The sort of behaviour we commonly see in Parliament is quite unprofessional and unacceptable. Courtesy and truthfulness should be mandatory.

10. *Comprehensive and continual training in policy, ethics and procedures for MPs and ministerial staff.* Staff development is common in the commercial world, so it should be for politicians.

11. *Commit to stronger regulation of lobbyists.* Do we need lobbyists at all, as a profession? It is undemocratic. All people should have equal access to politicians, not just those who can afford a lobbyist to jump the queue for them.

12. *Independent selection process for senior appointments to the Australian Public Service, the judiciary and major statutory bodies.* Absolutely. Otherwise conflicts of interest and for instance climate deniers being appointed to environmental committees – as we do right now.

13. *Trial a citizen jury that would allow a small representative sample of the community to explore a major national issue in depth.* Definitely. Citizens' assemblies (see below) could play a vital role. How mandatory should their conclusions be?

14. *Lead a national conversation to renew Australian democracy and update the Constitution.* The Constitution certainly needs looking at but it opens a huge question about what needs changing and whether a bill of rights should be incorporated. I discuss that below (16).

15. *Lead a national conversation about the operation of the Australian Federation.* We need to clarify the roles of Commonwealth, states and

territories, even though this is likely to open a can of worms. No harm in a 'conversation' but whether that would lead to agreed action is a very different matter.

If both left and right ex-politicians like Brumby and Newman can agree on all these above proposals, maybe, just maybe, many of them could be implemented within the present system. But it would have to be bipartisan and that is not where the Morrison government is ever likely to be.

I would add further proposals

16A. *A Bill of Rights.* A Bill of Rights (BoR) is a list of the fundamental rights of citizens of a country. It exists to protect the rights of individuals from being violated by the state or by other individuals. A BoR can be entrenched or unentrenched. An entrenched BoR is contained within the constitution of the country, meaning it cannot be changed by an act of parliament but only by referendum. An unentrenched BoR is an ordinary act of parliament which can be altered or repealed by parliament.[79] An entrenched BoR is what this country needs, otherwise it can be changed, Abbott-like, by following governments. The most common argument against a BoR, especially by politicians, is that parliament is elected where a court is not and therefore an entrenched BoR is giving too much power to an unelected body. But take what happened when Boris Johnson became prime minister of the UK; he was deemed to have behaved illegally by the Supreme Court by misleading the Queen. In other words, an entrenched body of principle and law is more consistently democratic in matters of dispute than a government of the day because it rules for all, whereas a rogue PM, president or a senior minister would rule for their own benefit. But whatever form of BoR, citizens' rights need to stated clearly, what they are entitled to, such as housing, food, equality before the law and a right to a fair trial (which would need adequate legal aid, which we don't have at present). Otherwise the government of the day can do what they like to people they disapprove of. As indeed is happening in Australia today in the Witness K case.

16B. *A formal Aboriginal voice to Parliament.* Enough of bogus claims that this would amount to a third chamber. It too would need to be entrenched in the Constitution as for a BoR. In fact, it could be incorporated in a Bill of Rights.

17. *Strong anti-corruption laws.* Under pressure, the Morrison government set up a Commonwealth Integrity Commissioner (CIC); under that person will be a Law Enforcement Integrity Commissioner and a Public Sector Integrity Commissioner. However, it had limited powers, all hearings to be conducted in secret, and with too much ministerial discretion clogging the system. The very point of such laws should be that they are totally transparent, that they are independent and have teeth that bite. The Independent Commission Against Corruption (ICAC) formed in Hong Kong in 1974 did have real teeth and it transformed a grossly corrupted polity into a law-abiding one, but all that is being undermined by the Chinese jumping the gun on the One Country Two Systems agreement. This original ICAC was used by Nick Greiner to form the NSW version in 1988. What we need is the same at federal level but Morrison rejected that in favour of the weaker CIC.

18. *Whistle-blower protection.* This is absolutely vital where governmental or other wrong doing is perceived. If the whistle-blower(s) act for personal motives such as revenge, then that can be tested and appropriate legal action taken against them. However, when whistle-blowing uncovers serious wrongdoing, especially by government, then it is in the public interest to expose it. The prosecution of Witness K and his lawyer in the bugging of the East Timor government office by government agents for the benefit particularly of private Australian company Woodside is particularly heinous, especially as national security was falsely invoked as a defence.

19. *In election campaigns all aspiring politicians and parties must state and clearly explain their policies.* It is not good enough in a democracy to refuse to say where a politician and his/her party stand for on important issues.

20. *Reduce ministerial discretion.* Increasingly, individual ministers

and especially the Minister for Home Affairs have too much discretion over people's lives. Even Scott Morrison disagreed with his AG Christian Porter when he said that prosecutions should not be on the whim of politicians, but his solution was to toughen laws even further as in the press freedom cases.

These twenty proposals could be brought about without any major structural difference to government. If they were enacted, they would greatly change the nature of government and most importantly the sort of the people elected to office. They could provide major changes that could well expedite progress on more basic structural changes – if indeed they would be needed by then

Four foci of good governance

As mentioned in Chapter 1, good governance in today's society needs to involve at least these four areas of concern:

1. growing the economy;
2. legislating for the social good of all citizens;
3. maintaining environmental sustainability; and
4. being a good global citizen, dealing peaceably and equitably with other nations.

Good governance means addressing a reasonable balance between these concerns. For example, focusing too heavily on growing the economy using non-renewable resources is not sustainable, nor is it likely to be fair to large groups of citizens or to other countries. The sort of national populism that Trump and now Scott Morrison champion is quite incompatible with being a good global citizen.

These emphases are relative. Scandinavian countries have free market economies but high taxes provide good social welfare that benefits all citizens. In most neoliberal countries, this is not the case. Taxes are cut and so social services wither; growth economies using non-renewable resources inevitably means the environment suffers.

What form of government would best achieve optimal balance amongst these areas of concern?

The two-party Westminster system

Two-party government emerged from the simpler world of the eighteenth century, giving rise to the Westminster system of government. Australian politics still follows this general model despite the existence of minor parties and independents. A majority government of Labor or Liberal is considered the right way for the system to work, and where that doesn't happen parliament is said to be 'hung', as if the life of good governance is slowly being strangled.

However, where one major party has an absolute majority in both houses, they are in effect granted open slather to do whatever they want to do: the opposition and other MPs are simply dealt out of the game until next election. As one-time Tasmanian Premier Paul Lennon put it, he had a mandate to do whatever he thought best for Tasmania and if Tasmanians didn't like it, they could chuck him out at the next election. He is not the only politician to confuse democracy with serial autocracy.

When it comes to the crunch in our system, only cabinet, or the prime minister alone, have any real decision-making power. The rank and file almost always back what the inner few decide. In that case, backbenchers, who are supposed to represent their electorate, are a waste of space and resources. If all backbenchers were sacked, it would hardly make a difference to parliamentary outcomes. And just think of the money saved if all those redundant politicians were sacked! Of course, backbenchers could have a most important role in government in committee work developing and refining policies, engaging with the community, and much else, but as things currently stand, we have government by oligarchy at the cost of government by democracy. When one party rules both houses, this is not even a two-party system but one-party rule, with the defeated party sniping away ineffectually at the sidelines.

The preselection of candidates in the two-party system is intrinsically undemocratic. We ordinary voters are forced to vote for the candidates that have been preselected for us, not for the candidate we think might best represent us. Our elections and Chinese elections are the same in this respect. The people of Hong Kong vote for candidates selected by Beijing, who will behave as Beijing dictates. Western countries rightly decry this, but many Western countries do exactly the same, Australia especially. Preselected candidates vote the way they are told to, just as Hong Kong politicians do – unless they are indeed brave, as some are.

This virtually unchecked power of the ruling party clearly opens the door to corruption because it provides a focus for lobbying and political donations that are intended to influence decision-making. Massive donations to the Liberal Party in Tasmania by gambling giant Federal Hotels saw that government returned in the 2018 state election after a record of incompetence, doing secret deals for developer mates (commercial-in-confidence, you see) and general negligence. Labor stood on a platform of restricting poker machines to casinos: that was their undoing. Despite the fact that some 70% of the population wanted poker machines banned from pubs and clubs, a massive advertising campaign by Federal, running into undisclosed millions, undermined Labor. Big money had crushed the popular will. On the federal front, there is no doubt at all, despite shrill denials by Coalition ministers, that massive donations by the fossil fuel industry to both parties, especially to the Liberal Party, are behind the push to open more coal mines, including Adani. In multiparty governments, if no one party has this kind of power, corruption is less likely.

The difference between the parties in a two-party system is basically a left-right divide, but the factions within a party also follow a left-right divide – or in the case of the Liberals an extreme right-moderate right divide. Such dichotomies are not a good fit to a society in which large subgroups of people have different concerns, needs and values. There are other important things that good governance of our complex society needs to attend to: climate change, mass migration, the catastrophic implications of nuclear war, corporatisation that straddles national borders, cheap foreign labour creating unemployment in first world countries and pillaged resources in the developing world, diminishing non-renewable resources when there is increasing demand for them. Handling all these and many other issues is beyond the competence of a two-party system, where the chief preoccupation is for each party to argue that the other side's solutions are wrong. Bipartisan support used to occur but is rare today, except shamefully on the treatment of asylum seekers and for the faux bipartisanship created by wedging. Internal corruption of policy creation by wedging is a pathology that is invited by two-party government.

Wedging has been a time-honoured tactic in two-party governments. The Coalition has been particularly effective in wedging craven Labor leaders by invoking terrorism and national security when neither is in question, but Labor dare not appear to be weak on such issues. Howard was a master at this, forcing Labor in its weakness to support cruel asylum seeker policies. By July 2019, some eighty-two bills had been enacted attacking freedom of speech and human rights, and granting powers to police and ASIO that have been equalled only in time of war. When Labor has called for bipartisanship on a matter of national importance, the Coalition have typically responded with wedging, forcing Labor to adopt policies that are contrary to Labor's traditional values. This is a serious fault that two-party systems of government seem prone to.

The present government is an example where internal forces within a party distort what the party stands for. The hard-right members of the present government in the House of Representatives are not even representative of their own party let alone the voters who elected them. Of the total of seventy-seven Coalition members, about twenty are from the hard right, less than a third of the total, yet this minority sets the tone for the whole government. The answer is that preselection by the Liberal Party by the divisions in the organisational wing of the party tends to favour enough hard-right candidates to be elected and then selected for cabinet and other posts by the prime minister, himself from the hard right. Thus is the party line established. The remaining moderate majority follow that line or they will find themselves out of a job. Party politics doesn't sit well with representation within democracy itself or even within the party. The Coalition in short has been hijacked by the extreme right.

Party rule, most insistent in two-party governments, is a problem in a democracy: the power of the party to force members to stick to what the party room has decided, or else. As independent federal MP Andrew Wilkie wrote,

> Even the best of people with the best of intentions can struggle in a party environment… Examples of party members failing to follow their consciences, or to effectively represent their constituencies, are many but none are more striking than the parliamentary votes on asylum seekers…and animal welfare. Time and time again otherwise good people have been on the public record making principled statements…then walked into the Chamber, sat with their party and made a complete mockery of their previous behaviour. If I could make just one change to the way Australia does politics, it would be to somehow enforce the right of every parliamentarian, to vote in accordance with their conscience and their constituency's wishes.[80]

In the UK and the US, crossing the floor is no big deal, but it is specifically ruled out in the ALP; although technically allowable in Liberal, National and Greens, politicians vote against their own party at their peril. Very simple: they won't be preselected come the next election. Independents don't face this problem.

Indeed, voters themselves are turning away from both major parties. Last figures (from Google) for the Liberals was 80,000 in 2018 and 50,000 for Labor in 2018. This is compared to hundreds of thousands of members for both parties decades ago. On the other hand, new minor parties and independents members are increasing. On these sorts of figures, the two-party system seems to be losing popular support.

Multiparty or power-sharing government

The power and interests of any one party dwindle in the presence of several other parties, allowing politicians to concentrate more on legislating for the interests of the people they represent rather than on legislating in the party interest. Legislative decisions have to be made through discussion and negotiation between parties, a procedure that focuses on producing outcomes that have been discussed from different perspectives and that suit a diverse electorate. Legislation is therefore more carefully considered and nuanced than in two-party systems, the consequences of proposed legislation being studied and analysed.

The design of the parliament reflects these differences between two-party and multiparty systems. In Westminster systems, the two parties face each other across a divide, which invites confrontation. Scandinavian politicians, however, sit in a semicircle facing a president; changing the seating arrangements along these lines was included in the Melbourne University recommendations (see above).

In Norway, the unicameral parliament has 169 members, and is elected every four years, based on proportional representation. There is no upper house, but where people trust their parliamentarians, an upper house of review in order to keep the bastards honest is deemed unnecessary. It also allows legislation to take effect quickly, whereas in Australia a negative Senate can stall legislation and governance itself – but when the legislation is hasty and poorly conceived, it should be stalled and reconsidered. In Denmark, electioneering is limited to three weeks, which means that for the greater part of the year politicians can get on with governing rather than scoring points in election-mode the year round. And short election campaigns save a lot of money.

Scandinavian systems are multiparty power-sharing systems so that issues are discussed and negotiated from different angles of interest, not just that of the currently dominant party. The outcomes are better – including economic outcomes; the citizens are happier and, compared to other Western countries, the politicians are more trusted.[81] Scandinavian politicians are probably not more honest or less corruptible as people than are Australian politicians, but the structures of their respective systems elicit or encourage quite different kinds of behaviour.

New Zealand, like Scandinavian countries, does not have an upper house. This puts pressure on politicians to get it right first time, which may account for the mood of cooperation between parties. But that is not how it would work in Australia. Imagine Tony Abbott sitting down with Julia Gillard to work things through cooperatively, or Scott Morrison with Bill Shorten! The fact that we do have an upper house is precisely because we feel we need a check on goodness knows what horrors an unchecked lower house might get up to. Practically speaking, a one-house system, almost always in New Zealand in an alliance with a minor party, means that they avoid problems with an upper house. In our case, the upper house virtually crippled the Abbott and Turnbull governments – and just as well. To complicate the picture, our federal government has to contend with states, the Senate supposedly a states' house, which does not apply to New Zealand. So all up, a New Zealand government has a clearer path to take in running the country.

Could the personalities of our respective politicians and leaders have anything to do with the importance of an upper house? After the confrontational Piggy Muldoon, New Zealand has had a number of good leaders, both National (Conservative) and Labor, starting with David Lange, who stood up to US bullying with his refusal to allow nuclear-armed ships into New Zealand waters, a policy that New Zealand continues to this day. The policy surely displeased the United States and Australia, but it pleased New Zealanders no end. Helen Clark was the first female prime minister and had three terms; her strong points were international relations and social welfare.

John Key was a strong neoliberal; he kept the budget in surplus but maintained social welfare and housing programmes. He must have been a nice guy, for he was popular with both sides of politics. If 'niceness' is an issue in politics, perhaps it is significant that strong neoliberal governments like Key's can still take a humane attitude to asylum seekers. They offered to take some of our Manus and Nauru detainees, which is what our government wanted, but they still refused because those terrible asylum seekers might then come in to Australia via the Tasman backdoor. That alone tells us who the nice guys are and who are the bastards.

Political commentator Laura Tingle notes,

> In countries from Norway to New Zealand…minority government [has] become a permanent feature of the political landscape. New Zealand's political parties have had to strike very different negotiating arrangements, and accept that they have to work, long before policy options come up before parliament. The result is pragmatism rather than 'oppositionism'…while Australia's capacity to conduct a grown-up debate about almost anything has stalled.[82]

Let us look briefly at alternative systems that work on issues rather than on party politics.

Issues-based government

One alternative system of government minimises party rule by governing on issues. Something like issues-based government exists in Hong Kong, or rather used to exist but things are changing fast there and it is dangerous to generalise. Basically, the Legislative Council, which enacts legislation, comprises thirty-five members elected by citizens and who may be members of political parties, and thirty-five members elected by functional, occupation-based constituencies, such as education, health, business, transport, and so on. Decisions are made by politicians who are responsible for different sectors of the community, and are advised by experts on their respective portfolios. Our system of appointing a favoured politician (probably with a law degree) to the health portfolio seems in contrast just irresponsibly stupid, not to say arrogant on the part of the appointee to don the responsibility of making decisions in areas in which he or she is basically ignorant.

Elections can go horribly wrong as they did in the 2016 election that placed Trump in the Oval Office and in Australia in the elections of Abbott, as a protest against Labor's chaos, and again when the campaign was debased into a personality contest between Morrison and

175

Shorten. So is there an alternative to elections? Belgian writer David Van Reybrouck concludes,

> Elections are the fossil fuel of politics. Whereas once they gave democracy a huge boost, much like the boost oil gave the economy, it now turns out they cause colossal problems of their own.[83]

Reybrouck discusses an alternative to elections which goes back to ancient Greece, where citizens themselves (but males only) directly made decisions. That is not manageable in large populations but it is possible to use selected groups of citizens, as happens in juries in court trials. This form of issues-based government is called sortition, in which a panel of citizens is asked to consider a particular issue, reflect on evidence and arguments from both sides of the debate and reach a decision. The citizens could be empanelled in a variety of ways, the most democratic being random selection, but more reliability would involve a stratified representative sampling. The agenda of these citizens' assemblies could be drawn up through public consultation, or by an elected chamber.

Sortition curtails the power of political parties, because citizens would vote on issues on the basis of their reflections on submitted evidence, rather than being whipped into line by a party leader, as elected party members are. Sortition would limit the influence of career politicians, because members of citizens' assemblies would serve only once, making corruption distinctly less likely.

Contemporary versions of sortition could combine with an elected legislature. The lower house might be comprised of elected politicians; the upper house, the house of review, comprised of empanelled citizens would be quite independent of the lower house – as a house of review should be. We have had endless problems in Australia with a party-based Senate, especially when the governing party also has a majority in the Senate: then all sorts of bad legislation can be rushed through, as happened during John Howard's last term (and was largely responsible for his downfall). On the other hand, at worst a Senate comprising a non-government party majority can stall legislation rendering government ineffectual.

An advantage of sortition is its flexibility. Using representatives of ordinary people ensures legislation is continually contextualised so that it will be more in line with what people think and value, thus reflecting the ever-changing culture of society. In our current system career politicians can be quite out of touch with community thinking and values. The story of same sex marriage is a dramatic example of change in public thinking: a you've-got-to-be-joking view a decade ago is decidedly mainstream today, leaving conservative politicians way behind those they were supposed to be representing as they struggled to throw up obstructions to that legislation.

One worry with sortition-based decision-making is that it gives the experts who create the briefing materials the power to frame the assembly's discussions. A balanced and fair-minded compilation of evidence and arguments is the key for citizen-based decision-making, so this is an important challenge for advocates of sortition.

Small-scale examples have been used successfully in Canada, Bolivia and Denmark to provide input on particular issues. A particularly interesting example is a citizens' assembly on Brexit. In September 2017, a year after the actual Brexit referendum in the UK, a citizens' assembly was called by the Constitution Unit of the University College of London. It brought together fifty citizens randomly selected from thousands who reflected the diversity of the UK electorate in terms of age, gender, ethnicity, region, social class and views on Brexit. Meetings were held over two weekends, the first for learning about issues, the second for discussing and developing recommendations. The results were quite close to the original vote, a small majority for leaving the EU, but the options were far more nuanced and allowed for compromise. The 2016 referendum itself demanded a binary decision, leave/not leave, with no room for compromise. Fifty citizens is not enough of course, but this exercise was quick and cheap (the members of the assembly got all costs and an honorarium of £200) and still achieved a better, more nuanced, result than the referendum itself.[84]

Where Enlightenment thinking comes in

Let us go back to that question of what is a 'reasonable' balance between the four concerns a government should attend to. That balance must not be for the benefit of a select rich few, as it is in neoliberal governments; nor should it be for the benefit of a political party. It must be for the benefit of all citizens, including citizens of the global community. That is what is 'reasonable'. And the means by which that benefit is distributed is through fact, evidence and reasoned argument. In this way, we have both of the two dimensions of the Enlightenment in operation: reason and humanity.

The belief that all people are equal regardless of gender or ethnicity is ostensibly the foundation of democracy itself yet as we have seen many so-called democratic systems do not allow equality. For example, our two-party winner-takes-all system gives more power to one side of the polity – that side whose party is in majority government – than to those who voted for the opposition party. They must wait their turn to be in power. And for those who voted for neither party, tough luck. Preselection of candidates is usually done by party heavies and we lesser beings can only vote for those who have been selected for us to consider. When China does that for Hong Kong elections, we cry foul but that is exactly what happens in Australia.

Thus, the balance between those four components of governance, and how well we achieve that balance, depends very much on how seriously we take the Scandinavian notion of 'all men's rights'. According to that notion, people in remote areas get the same supports and infrastructure as people in large cities. Political parties alone cannot do the job of balancing priorities optimally. A multiparty system does this better than a two-party system but the combination of a multiparty system and a sortition-based citizens council working cooperatively seems a more promising way to go.

Changes in the culture of society have in the past been effected by leadership, particularly bipartisan leadership. This we saw work positively in the 1970s. With the White Australia Policy officially ending only in 1973, three years later we were accepting and resettling thousands of Vietnamese refugees in a bipartisan agreement. But in 1992, again in a bipartisan agreement under Paul Keating as PM, the rights of life, liberty, and the pursuit of happiness, not to mention recognition of international law, were thrown out the window and mandatory detention was introduced for boat arrivals. This has worsened since, most notably through Minister Dutton stirring up racial hatreds, such as his beat-up about African gangs that terrorise respectable Melburnians as they go to restaurants.[85] This extraordinary series of turnarounds in only a few years is perhaps an indication of how powerful political leadership can be.

Those turnarounds occurred in a two-party system and depended too much on the personalities of the leaders who happened to be around at the time. Our major difficulty at the moment is that party structures encourage conflict and nastiness between politicians and the trickledown effect from that to the electorate is not good, producing either cynicism about all politicians or the message that shouting insults is the way to conduct business. Neither is likely to achieve a stable culture change in positive directions. Gaining leadership itself is too often a matter of bullying and lying, and of course money.

We are undoubtedly in a bad space at the time of writing but this review would suggest that under the right government, with enlightened and Enlightenment thinking, we can do much better. A system that evolves from within society, as discussed previously in the twenty proposals (pages 164–168), that represents the different sections of society as much as possible, would be a more stable and more informed body with which to provide leadership than leaving it to party factional leaders.

As to the much more complex issue of changing the system away from our present two-party Westminster-style system, I would leave it until our present government is in better shape.

But however we handle it, my earnest wish is that this book may contribute to more reasoned decision-making and a cooperative polity instead of one that is based on confrontation, party interest and self-interest.

References and Notes

Introduction

1. First published in *Tasmanian Times*, 1 January 2014.
http://tasmaniantimes.com
/index.php?/articleindex/p11400
/P2640

Chapter 1

2. Given to the Global Warming Policy Foundation on 5 November 2013. This foundation is a right-wing think tank committed to countering the 'extremely dama-ging and harmful policies' envis-aged by governments to mitigate anthropogenic global warming.
3. *The Guardian*, 25 July 2012.
4. Jean Parker, *Solidarity*, October 2012.
http://www.solidarity.net.au/50/
labors-accord-how-hawkeand-
keating-began-a-neoliberal-
revolution/
5. *Sydney Morning Herald*, 30 March 2017.
6. Thomas Piketty, *Capital in the Twenty First Century*, Harvard University Press, 2014.
7. Antonio Gramsci, *Prison Notebooks (1929–35)*, Columbia University Press, 1992.
8. Richard Denniss, 'Econo-babble: how to decode political spin and economic nonsense', Schwartz, *Redback Quarterly*, No. 8, 2016.
9. More general deliberate obfuscations can be found in Don Watson's *Dictionary of Weasel Words*, Random House, 2011.
10. George Monbiot, 'This transatlantic trade deal is a full-frontal assault on democracy', *The Guardian*, 5 November 2013.
11. https://crawford.anu.edu.au/
pdf/ajrc/wpapers/2015/201501.
pdf
12. http://www.abc.net.au/news/
2018-01-29/why-the-tpp-was-
revived-without-donald-trump/
9368736
13. P. Willans, 'Turning politicians into corporate servants', *Tasmanian Times*, 19 November 2013.
http: //tasmaniantimes.com/
index.php?/weblog/article/
turning-politicians-into-
corporateservants-/show_
comments

14. John Ralston Saul, 'The reinvention of the world – lt's broke: How can we fix it?', The University of Tasmania, 27 August, 2012.

15. Richard Denniss, 'Dead Right: How neoliberalism has eaten itself and what comes next', *Quarterly Essay*, Issue 70, 2018.

16. Greg Barns, *Rise of the Right: The War on Australia's Liberal Values*, Hardie Grant, 2019.

17. *The Age*, 14 July 2014.

18. https://www.nobelprize.org/ceremonies/archive/speeches/opening-2016.html

Chapter 2

19. Bill Bryson, *Down Under*, Black Swan Books, 2000, p. 120.

Chapter 3

20. https://en.wikipedia.org/wiki/Fascism

21. *Independent Australia*, 13 May 2014. http://www.independentaustralia.net/politics/politicsdisplay/what-if-abbott-and-his-cronies-are-just-a-bunch-of-psychopaths,6472

22. See at https://www.youtube.com/watch?v=9wT9XS TvzQ

23. Goebbels wrote, 'The most brilliant propagandist technique will yield no success unless one fundamental principle is borne in mind constantly – it must confine itself to a few points and repeat them over and over.' This quote is also attributed to Adolf Hitler.

24. https://www.jewishvirtuallibrary.org/jsource/Holocaust/goebbelslie.html

25. Alan Austin, http://www.independentaustralia.net/politics/politics-display/is-australia-run-bycompulsive-liars-part-two-abbotts-astonishing-30-lies,6398

26. https://www.youtube.com/watch?v= Tc51jcri6Nk

27. *The Monthly*, November 2013.

28. https://www.youtube.com/watch?v=c31aKVmkXuk

29. As an aside, we could run Trump's administration against the criteria of fascism:
• a strong leader or small group of leaders with psychopathic tendencies;
• a culture of lying;
• rules by fiat and slogan;
• defines and maintains an underclass while redistributing wealth and power to an elite;
• filters information so that the government only receives advice it wants to hear;
• controls the media;
• nationalistic and militaristic;
• is a poor world neighbour;
• takes over industry and commerce;
• proposes to establish through violence a new ultra-nationalistic order.

A strong 'yes' to all, even the last. The violence is already there and the way Trump is defying the press and the law courts he does seem to be heading towards a new ultra-nationalistic order.

30. Niki Savva, *The Road to Ruin: How Tony Abbott and Peta Credlin Destroyed their own Government*, Scribe, 2016.
31. *Australian*, 7 April 2018.

Chapter 4

32. Alan Austin, 'Corruption and incompetence escalate on Turnbull's watch', *Independent Australia*, 31 December 2015.
33. https://independentaustralia. net/ politics/politics-display/ corruption-andincompetence-esca late-on- turnbulls-watch,853333. https://www.abcnet.au/news/ 2016-11-22/turnbull-praises- dutton-amid-comments-about lebanese-community/8047038
34. https://theconversation.com/ grattan-on-friday-has-turnbulls- credibility-deficit-reached-a- pointof-no-return-70144? utm_medium=email&utm_ campaign=Latest%20from%20 The%20Conversation%20for% 20December%209%202016% 20-%206259&utm_content= Latest%20from%20The%20 Conversation%20for%20 December%209%202016%20- %206259+CID_
3d53640e26fff6c7b34e37d4c65e fd0a&utm_source=campaign_ monitor&utm_term=Grattan% 20on%20Friday%20Has%20 Turnbulls%20credibility%20 deficit%20reached%20a%20 point% 20of%20no%20return *New Matilda*, 8 December.
35. https://envirojustice.org.au/ sites/default/files/files/ envirojustice_adani_ environmental report.pdf
36. *Australian*, 4 April 2017.
37. https://theconversation .com/marriage-eguality-lobby-an d-labor-must-decide-how-to-han dle-postalballot-82223?utm_ medium=email&utm_campaign =Latest%20from%20The%20 Conversation%20for<>lo20 August%209%202017%20-% 2080306435&utm_content= Latest%20from%20The%20 Conversation%20for%20August %209%202017%20-%2080306 435+CIDc2efd7559a235a0aae4 186d273143560&utm_source= campaign_monitor&utm_term= Malcolm%20Turnbull%20 invokes%20Me%20Tarzan%20 defence%20against%20postal% 20ballot%20criticism
38. *Mercury*, 31 May 2018.
39. Op. cit.
40. https://newmatilda.com/ 2016/ 12/02/a-badly-wounded- government-limps-to-the-long- summerbreak/

New Matilda, 2 December 2016.
41. https://www.theguardian.
com/australia-news/2018/jan/22
/top-1-per-cent-of-australians-
ownmore-wealth-than-bottom-
70-per-cent-combined
42. *Mercury,* 3 August 2017.

Chapter 5

43. George Megalogenis, 'The
Rookie PMs: How Canberra's
leadership circus is damaging ties
with Asia', *Australian Foreign
Affairs,* Issue 5, February 2019.
44. Taken from Hansard:
https://parlinfo.aph.gov.au/
parllnfo/search/display/display.
w3p;query=ld:%22chamber
/hansardr/2008-02-14/0045%22
45. Julian Burnside, *The Age,* 23
December 2014.
46. Behrouz Boochani, *No
Friend but the Mountains,*
Picador, 2018.
47. https://independentaustralia.
net/politics/politics-display/scott
-morrison-and-the-pentecostal-
one-world-government-dogma,
13306
48. https://www.google.com/
search?q=Harvard+Divinity+Sch
ooi+Religious+Uteracy+Project&
rlz=1C1CHBF enGB&oq=
Harvard+Divinity+Schooi+
Religious+Literacy+Project&aqs
=chrome..69i57.458610j0j4&
sourceid=chrome&ie=UTF-8
49. https://www.nationalreview.

com/corner/sources-poverty-
david-french/
50. Boyce, James. 'The Devil and
Scott Morrison: What do we
know about the prime minister's
Pentecostalism?', *The Monthly,*
February 2019.
51. Tanya Levin, 'Understand
Scott Morrison's Pentecostalism',
https://7ampodcast.com.au/
episodes/understanding-scott-
morrisons-pentecostalism
52. John Wren, 'Wren's Week:
Australia, the laughing stock of
the world', *Independent Australia,*
15 July 2019.
https://independentaustralia.net/
life/life-djsplay/wrens-week-
australia-the-laughingstock- of-
the-world,12894
53. Mark McKenna, 'The quiet
Australians: Just how silent does
Morrison want Australians to
be?', *The Monthly,* June 2019.
54. https://www. tai.org.au/sites/
default/files/P584%20Trickle%
200ut%20Effect.pdf
55. SBS News, 17 March 2019.
56. Jennifer Wilson, 'Morrison's
expedient condemnation of
Christchurch terror attack',
Independent Australia, 18 March
2019.
https://independent
australia.net/politics/politics-
display/morrisonsexpedient-
condemnation-of-christchurch-
terror-attack,l2480

57. Peter Boyer, 'Australia faces greenhouse gas blowout', *Mercury*, 5 March 2019.

58. Rob White, 'Killing a planet is a criminal act', *Mercury*, 6 March 2019

59. Paddy Manning, *The Monthly Today*, 6 March 2019.

60. Rebecca Huntley, 'Australia Fair: Listening to the nation', *Quarterly Essay*, Issue 73, 2019.

Chapter 6

61. Alan Austin, 'Top ten Budget deceptions, brought to you by Treasurer Josh Frydenberg', *Independent Australia*, 8 April 2019.

62. Erik Jensen, 'The Prosperity Gospel: How Scott Morrison won and Bill Shorten lost', *Quarterly Essay*, Issue 74, 2019.

63. Luke Metcalfe, 'Less educated Australians swung spectacularly to the Coalition', *Rapid Intelligence*, 19 May 2019.

64. Stephen Long, 'Inside Scott Morrison's Donald Trump-like election victory', ABC *Australia Votes*, 24 May 2019.

65. John Wren, 'A look inside Morrison's dirty Cabinet', Independent Australia, 31 May 2019.

66. https://www.abc.net.au/news/2019-05-19/annabel-crabb-election-result-2019-scott-morrisonmandate/11127994

67. https://en.m.wikipedia.org/wiki/Mandate_(politics)

68. https://www.theguardian.com/commentisfree/2017/dec/30/when-it -comes-to-refugees-abbottturnbull-morrison-and-dutton-are-hypocrites

69. https://tasmaniantimes.com/2018/04/the-paradox-of-christianitv-right-or-left-wing/

70. https ://www. righttoknow. org.au/

71. Jill Locke, *Democracy and the Death of Shame*, Cambridge University Press, 2016.

72. lan Dunt on *Late Night Live*, ABC Radio National, 25 September 2019.

73. Margaret Simons, *Penny Wong: Passion and Principle*, Black Inc, 2019.

74. *The Guardian*, 14 October 2019.

Chapter 7

75. George Grundy, https://independentaustralia.net/politics/politics-display/the-global-rise-ofrightwing-authoritarianism, 13232

76. James Walter, 'The mischief of Australian Democracy', *Island Magazine*, Issue 136, 2014.

77. https://theconversation.com/australians-trust-in-politicians-and-democracy-hits-an-all-time-l ownew-research-108161

78. https://www.abc.net.au/news/2019-05-07/federal-electio n-2019-sees-ideas-pitched-to-reformdemocracy/11082216

79. https://www.gotocourt.com.au/legal-news/australia-bill-of-rights/

80. Andrew Wilkie, 'Independence Day', *Island Magazine*, Issue 136, 2014.

81. https://www.google.eom.au/search?q=Transparency+International&oq=Transparency+International&aqs=chrome..69i57.7914482j0j3&sourceid=chrome&es_sm=122&ie=UTF-8

82. Laura Tingle, 'Wicked Problems: the rise and stall of Malcolm Turnbull', *The Monthly*, May 2017, p. 27.

83. Peter van Reybrouck, *Against Elections: The Case for Democracy*. Penguin Random House, 2016.

84. https://citizensassembly.co.uk/brexit/about/

85. Peter Brent, 'Peter Dutton for Prime Minister!', *Inside Story*, 12 January 2018.

www.ingramcontent.com/pod-product-compliance
Lightning Source LLC
Chambersburg PA
CBHW030246030426
42336CB00009B/286

* 9 7 8 1 7 6 0 4 1 8 8 2 3 *